ICT & HIGHER EDUCATION

DR. SAVITA MISHRA

Copyright © Dr. Savita Mishra
All Rights Reserved.

This book has been published with all efforts taken to make the material error-free after the consent of the author. However, the author and the publisher do not assume and hereby disclaim any liability to any party for any loss, damage, or disruption caused by errors or omissions, whether such errors or omissions result from negligence, accident, or any other cause.

While every effort has been made to avoid any mistake or omission, this publication is being sold on the condition and understanding that neither the author nor the publishers or printers would be liable in any manner to any person by reason of any mistake or omission in this publication or for any action taken or omitted to be taken or advice rendered or accepted on the basis of this work. For any defect in printing or binding the publishers will be liable only to replace the defective copy by another copy of this work then available.

Contents

Preface

Education is the importance thing for our better life, a good education is extremely essential for everyone to grow and succeed in life, and it help in the growth of human civilization. Education is necessary to understand the universe around us and convert it into something more beneficial. With the help of knowledge, we can develop a new perspective for our life. In simple word we can say that education is the process of facilitating learning, or the acquisition of knowledge, skills, values, morals, beliefs, and habits.

Higher education facilitates quality learning all through the life among people of any age group, cast, creed, religion and region. Higher education is the process of achieving knowledge, values, skills, beliefs, and moral habits. People need to get high level awareness about the importance of knowledge more than before. In today's generation higher education is very necessary for each and every individual in order to improve knowledge, skills, life styles, as well as social and economic status throughout the life.

Information and Communication Technologies (ICT) refers to technologies which are used for collecting, storing, editing and spending on information in various forms. ICT enable the transformation of teaching, research and learning processes in the least levels. It empowers teachers and students, making significant contributions to the education fraternity. The ICT has been organized in several courses consistent with the goal, purpose and area of applicability. What is being learned also depends on the sort of education and therefore the level of the scholars. Education prepares students for the utilization of ICT in education, future occupation and social life.

Dr. Savita Mishra

CHAPTER ONE

ICT AND HIGHER EDUCATION

1.0. Introduction

The World Health Organization (WHO) declared Covid-19 as a pandemic on March 11, 2020. This Covid-19 (coronavirus) pandemic is not only a global health problem but also has severe impacts on human and social life, including employment, education, agriculture and the other spheres of the world economy. Due to the outbreak of Covid-19 Government announced a lockdown from 25th March of 2020 and extended it with adding more relaxations. The educational Institutions throughout the nation had never got any relaxation to start their educational activities during all phases of lockdown. Thus the education system is highly affected by the pandemic. Higher Education Institutions (HEIs), including universities, colleges and other institutions in tertiary education, are no exception. In many Institutions campuses are closed, terminal exams get postponed and the teaching learning process moved online. Transitioning from traditional face-to-face learning to online learning can be an entirely different experience for the Learners and the educators, which they adapt to with little or no other alternatives available.The coronavirus has terrifically affected everyone and made life hard to survive. The sharp pang of this virus has exponentially swept globally and has triggered fear, frustration, stress, and worried each one on earth. The pandemic brought in pernicious impacts on cognitive functions, physical and mental health. It has further shattered our daily routine, lifestyle, and all activities across disciplines. The sudden closure of schools, colleges, and universities globally has dictated the virtual delivery of courses and programs. Despite numerous inevitable teething problems, the researcher experiences if the future might just have become the present.

The first case of covid-19 was reported in India (Kerala) on 30 January 2020, originating from China. India has been experiencing sparkled growth in Covid-19 cases. As on 26 June 2020, India has reported 189463 active cases, 285636 recovered cases and 15301death cases. Experts suggest the number of infections could be much higher as India's testing rates are among the lowest in the world. The infection rate of covid-19 in India is reported to be 1.7, significantly lower than in the most horrible affected countries. The outbreak has been declared an epidemic in more than a dozen states and union territories, where provisions of the Epidemic Diseases Act, 1897, have been invoked, and educational institutions and many commercial establishments have been shut down. India has suspended all tourist visas, as a majority of the confirmed cases were linked to other countries. On 22 March 2020, India observed a 14-hour voluntary public curfew at the instance. The government followed it up with lockdowns in 75 districts where covid-19 cases had occurred as well as all major cities. Further, on 24 March, the prime minister ordered a nationwide lockdown for 21 days, affecting the entire 1.3 billion population of India. The World Health Organization chief executive director of health emergencies programme Michael Ryan says that India had "tremendous capacity" to deal with the corona virus outbreak and, as the second most populous country, will have enormous impact on the world's ability to deal with it.

Entry of Covid-19 in West Bengal: The first case (the 18-year-old student, who had returned from London) of the corona virus pandemic was confirmed in the West Bengal on 17 March, 2020. The state has confirmed a total of 15648 cases; including 606 deaths and 10190 recover as on 26 June, 2020.

The sudden arise of Covid 19 pandemic directly affect the education sectors like all the field of country's development. It affect the child's development and well being by segregate them from institution, ignored them by denying RTE norms and increase the inequalities which can foster the dropout and create the barrier for getting free and compulsory education. In this Home isolation period when all institutions were shutdown their door in all over the world, where continue of education became questionable, online learning overcoming the so called barrier for education like issue related to teacher, institution, distance, location etc. And make the education easily accessible in this period. Within a shortage and unnoticed time the stake holders change their track and trying to bring the all students in online based learning platform, so that, they smoothly continue their teaching learning process. This type of sudden shift from synchronous to asynchronous, traditional to online based teaching learning can create the adverse effect on the education system mainly the first learner, backward and rural learner. One third of children are unable to access the quality education due to the reason of digital divide (UNICEF, 2020). Comparing between the developed and the developing countries, it was significantly found that developing countries are facing more challenges such as poor internet connectivity, untrained ICT related personnel and weakness of content development than the developed countries (Aung T.N et. al, 2015).

Covid-19 has shaken up the global education enormously. Government is obliged to shut down the schools, colleges and universities across the whole nation due to mitigate the expansion of the novel corona virus. There was no assurance about the reopening of the educational institution. Natural perturbation of the lives of human beings has been stopped for an uncertain period. There was no immediate accomplishment to restrain the enormous outbreak of covid-19 for a precarious period as corona virus has impersonated a pandemic. Consequently, students of every level are obstructed to cease their class and stay at home for unlimited time. The entire commotion of the human being has run up for an unrestricted period. The whole education system has been closed for an uncertain period of time. Corona virus has proved this time as crucial for the education sector. All the activities related to education have been chocked up. Only a little number of private institutions were able to receive the online teaching learning method to continue the academic activities. It was not possible for the low income private and government institutions to adopt suddenly the online teaching learning method. There is a need of an immediate measure to ensure the continuity of the teaching learning process of government schools, colleges and universities. So the whole education system has been shifted from traditional to digital learning mode. Online learning is the best solution to overcome the critical pandemic situation. Government has initiated the digital version as a vital tool for accomplishing the present crisis due to covid-19. MHRD, Central government and State government have undertaken proper initiatives and have prepared diverse arrangements. The universities are unconditionally attempting to reduce the problem by adopting different digital technologies. The proper utilization of digital media should be prioritized for generating more advantageous position for millions of young students in India. Digital learning is more beneficial than traditional mode of learning. It has no geographical and physical boundary. Teachers also have performed their responsibilities for ensuring the learners engagement in online learning mode. They acted as the best guide and motivator for students. They have proved their competencies thoroughly during pandemic situation. There are enormous challenges for students and teachers to shift from offline to online teaching process. Various stakeholders and private organization have taken positive part to assist each other by inaugurating the online learning platform and exchange online app. Covid-19 pandemic has immersed one of the most oft-used terms 'new normal'. The significance of new normal in education system gives emphasis on impetuous usage of online learning tools. For many educational institutions, virtual learning has been reached as entire new normal mode of learning.

Education is in fact, one of great importance towards national development and Higher Education, in particular, plays a pivotal role in building up a powerful knowledge based society. It is always a key factor in incorporating changes and progress in the society. Since in a society, population compromises both men and women, so, according to the Constitution of India, Right to Education is equally important for women as well as men to prove their competitiveness in different of job fields in the global economy; as a quality education is like that of a life time opportunity of a woman which helps her to build up a strong personality so as to work and line in an increasingly competitive world education. It is that knowledge in women which will prove to be most powerful driving force in rapidly changing globalized economy and society and thereby also will help in reducing poverty and gender inequality in every spheres of life. Hence more enrolment of women in education particularly in higher education will enhance the competitiveness in the global economy.

The Indian higher education system has emerged as one of the largest system in the world with 14.6 million students enrolled in more than 31,000 institutions. Education is an essential element for the growth and prosperity of both a nation and society. Apart from primary and secondary education, higher education is optional for development and transformation of a conservative underdeveloped society. Higher Education has the omnipotent power of preparing future personalities in different spheres of life-social, economic, political, cultural, scientific and technical. According to UNESCO Report on education in the 21st century, Higher Education is a mandatory rule to bridge the knowledge gap between countries and communities so as to enrich mixing of culture, network of ideas research and technologies, in order to progress the lifeline of a backward society through the path of immense knowledge, research and development. Thus, Higher Education, if somehow enriched among women in society, can inevitably, provide the competencies that are required in different spheres of women activity, ranging from an administration to household, business, industry, health and tele communication and thereby extending to the arts and culture.

Out of 1.21 billion population in India, around 234 million fall in the age group of 15 – 24 years, which is expected to increase by 13% over 2005-2020 as compared to the world average of 4%. Hence, India is a potential area for the enhancement of higher education sector. India's education and training sector is estimated to be about US $40billion mark, with a potential women involvement (Annual Reports, Department of Higher Education).

Since independence, the growth of Indian higher education structure has undergone a remarkable transition and is a result of the nation's policy. It has been adopted immediately after independence, to promote education system in the country. Despite that, there is still an urge among women in the country to receive better higher education facilities, which has been measured in terms of enrolment in under graduation (also known as UG level) and under post graduation (also known as PG level) streams of educational institutions.

The years 2009-2010 to 2018-2019 have been chosen to differentiate between the role of women in higher education system in terms of their right to education according to Fundamental Rights as per laid down in Constitution of India. But, unfortunately, a pandamic of COVID-19 had started in the year of 2019-2020 and is still experiencing, with the outbreak of corona virus in the universe, including India, which had adversely affected and almost destructed the entire Indian economy. The entire world economy has been pushed into a state of ambiguity by this present disaster, which, has also led to the negative impacts on the most vital sectors such as agricultural sector, various industrial sectors (tourism & aviation, telecom, auto sector, transportation sectors) of the country. But the impact of COVID 19 on the education sector of the country was mixed (Agarwal et al, 2000).

Modern human civilization is facing a terrible virus around the world. The first attack of Corona virus in December 2019 in the wuhan province of China. On 9 January 2020 the issued a statement saying Chinese research has made preliminary determination of the virus as a novel corona virus.

The newly discovered virus is called COVID - 19 or Corona virus Disease. According to Health workers, the symptoms of this disease are mainly fever, and dry cough. It can also cause colds, sore throat, and diarrhea. This disease gradually spread one people to another people. Corona virus which is commonly called as covid-19 is an infectious disease which causes illness in the respiratory system in the humans. It is the new virus that is impacting the whole world badly as it is spreading primarily through contact with the person. The number of patients is increasing daily. It gradually spread another Chinese city. The virus also spreads Chinese to another country through the people, who are travel china to other country. Italy was the first attacked country after china. Then Covid – 19 has gradually spread to other countries like France, Spain, India, America etc. The Covid -19 virus has caused an epidemic around the world, which has stopped the pace of development of human life. In 2020 March 11, director general of WHO declared Covid - 19 is a global epidemic. In India, The first affected case of Corona virus was detected on 30 January 2020 in the state of Kerala and the affected had a Travel history from Wuhan, China. On March 14, the Indian government declared Covid – 19 a disaster. After 10 days March 24 announced a nationwide lockdown. From China to Britain, Italy to America, all the most developed and powerful countries in the world are helpless today.

Covid-19 is now a cause of large number of deaths across the world it spreads from person to person among those in close contact. Covid-19 attracted people; the most common symptoms are fever, dry cough, and breathing problem. Apart from this, symptoms like fatigue, sore throat, muscle pain, and loss of taste or smell can also be seen in corona virus patients.

The 1st phase of lockdown was announced by the Prime Minister on March 25, 2020 for 21 days. Then, the government of India has declared phase by phase lockdown. The markets have been closed; daily income of the people of village is completely stopped. The public is suffering a lot as a result of the lockdown.

Recently, people all over the world have been affected by Corona virus disease. With the overall cases worldwide rising rapidly the WHO has declared the outbreak a global health emergency. When the Indian government declared corona virus a disaster on March 14, Indians infected people of 82, Death 2. The government of India divides the country into Red, Orange, and Green Zone to prevent infection. This virus infects people of all ages; however older people are more likely to be infected. The virus is more prevalent in people with low immunity power. Gradually corona virus spread to different countries all over the world. The incidence of infection is not high in rural areas.

Higher education means tertiary education ruling to award of an academic degree. Higher education is also called post- secondary education, third level or tertiary education, is an optional final stage of formal learning that occurs after completion of secondary education. Higher education represent the level 6,7and 8 of the 2011 version of the International Standard Classification of Education structure. Tertiary education at a non-degree level is sometimes referred to as future education or continuing education as distinct from higher education. Higher education allows us to pursue a career that interests and inspires us. When we have the freedom to choose your career, we are more likely to enjoy it. Higher career or job satisfaction also comes from higher income, better employment benefits, and more advancement opportunities and responsibility. Higher education, any of various types of education students pursue in postsecondary institution of learning and usually affording, at the end of the course of study, a named "Degree", diploma or certificate of higher education and studies. Higher –educational institutions include not only universities and colleges but also various professional schools that provide preparation in such fields as law, theology, medicines, business, music, and art. Higher study also includes teacher-training schools, junior colleges, and institutes of technology. The basic entrance requirement for most higher-educational institutions is the completion of secondary education, and usual entrance age is about 18 years.

1.1. Covid 19 &Higher Education

Covid 19 is bringing several changes in Higher education. The effects of corona virus are undoubtedly a great loss. Covid 19 has the greatest impact on education. The Corona virus pandemic is not only a global health problem but also has severe impacts on human and social life, including employment, education, agriculture and the other region of the world economy.The covid – 19 pandemic shocked the world. Classes at educational institutions have been cancelled to reduce the outbreak of the growing corona virus. Educational institutions around the world have been forced to close their door. The pressure on students and higher education institutions has increased. Examinations in schools, colleges and universities have been postponed. Some examinations have been cancelled.

Virtual classes have been started in colleges and universities. There has been confusion about the admission of the academic year. According to UNESCO, more than 320 million students are currently affected in Indian schools and colleges. In the field of higher education, it has become necessary to give new continuity to the development of online platforms. But the socio – economic background of students in rural developing countries like India has a significant impact on higher education. Digital learning has widened this gap.

The announcement of a lock down all over India from March 24, 2020 has had a deeply effect on education in rural areas. The entire educational institute are totally close. The primary school and ICDS centre have also been developed as quarantine centres in the rural area. There is one of the alternative ways to continue the educational system is digital learning during this pandemic situation. This digital learning is done through various methods, like group calls, group chat, video conference, recorded voice etc. Apart from government sponsored resources, there are other e-learning platforms such as ZOOM, Google Meet, and WebEx which are interactive and can accessed from home.

But, all of this recent technology is unavailable in the rural area. For online studies, the most important things are the internet. But the internet's price is so high. So, the students of poor families are not to use this online education system. As a result, in the rural areas students are falling behind the urban areas student. This is the major effect of covid – 19 pandemic on higher education. There are several barriers to e-learning education system. Not all the people in the village have all the tools required for e-learning. Although internet service is now available in rural areas, it is a luxury for unemployed people at this time. So, not all students are able to take online education. As a result, they are lagging behind in this age of competition

The present education system of rural areas has become completely obsolete. Students have stopped studying at home as schools and colleges are closed. Many students have become involved in work due to lack of food. Although online classes have started in colleges and universities, most of them are being deprived of their opportunities. Not all students in the village have online class materials. Some students have smart phones but it is not possible to recharge during this lockdown period. Where there is a shortage of food in daily life, recharging and taking online classes is becoming a luxury. Although one or two students are attending online classes, there are still network problems. In villages where there is still no guarantee of electricity, it is becoming absolutely impossible to take online classes. If the education system was active, students could be much more aware through teachers. Students are also unable to be aware that the school is closed. If students were aware they could make their family members or people in the society aware.

1.1.1. Importance of Higher Education

First of all, Education gives the ability to read and write to anyone. Proper and good education is very important for all of us. Education is the importance thing for our better life, a good education is extremely essential for everyone to grow and succeed in life, and it help in the growth of human civilization. Education is necessary to understand the universe around us and convert it into something more beneficial. With the help of knowledge, we can develop a new perspective for our life. In simple word we can say that education is the process of facilitating learning, or the acquisition of knowledge, skills, values, morals, beliefs, and habits. Educational method includes teaching, training, storytelling, discussion and directed research. Higher education facilitates quality learning all through the life among people of any age group, cast, creed, religion and region. Higher education is the process of achieving knowledge, values, skills, beliefs, and moral habits. People need to get high level awareness about the importance of knowledge more than before. In today's generation higher education is very necessary for each and every individual in order to improve knowledge, skills, life styles, as well as social and economic status throughout the life. Getting proper education is the birth rights of everyone restricting which is the crime. Education is the ultimate way to get victory for over all personal and social problems. Education is very important to all of us as it plays very important roles in our life. In order to alive a better and peaceful life, we need to be educated. It transforms us completely from inside and outside by changing our mind and personality as well as improving our constructive in nature.

It helps a person to get knowledge and improves confidence level through the life. It plays a great role in our career growth as well as in the personal growth. It has no limitations, any age of people can get education at any stage of their life and anytime. It helps us to determine about good and bad things about our regular life. Higher educated person having good education become the good citizen in the society. We all want to see our kids going towards success which is only possible through the good and proper education. Every parent tells their kids from childhood about the importance of higher education in the life and all the advantage of education to make their mind towards better study in the future.

1. 2.Benefits of higher education for students

Higher education serves many purposes in our life, which are emphasized in our culture. Because we as a society do not acknowledge the full span of reason for achieving education after high schools or college, some young people may thinks it's not for them and therefore, miss out on many of the potential benefits that such an educational experience provides.

1. Career planning:

Career planning refers to the strategy a person uses to determine career goals and the path to achieve those goals. The process integrates various activities, including steps for self-improvement and the process of meeting these goals. The importance of career planning can't be over emphasized.

1. Broader practical benefits:

Preparing oneself for a career is not the only practical benefits of a college education. According to a 2013 reports by The College Board, there are many other important ones. Consider the following areas in which people with more than a high school diploma tend to be more successful in life.

3. Personal development:

It gives students a chance to develop attitude and skills that give them courage, ability to work with others and a better understanding of himself and the entire world around them. It is during college years that a person gets to understand his identity, role, dreams.

4. Pursuing a passion:

Pursuing a passion is the perhaps the least-accepted reason, culturally, to pursue higher education. Some hold that the time and financial investment of post-secondary school should only be pursued with practical, concrete career goals in mind. However, pursuing our passion is an extremely important component of a healthy, well-lived life.

2. Responsibilities of students in higher education during the Covid-19 pandemic and new normal period

The student has the most important part to play in education. The teacher would only be willing to teach if the student is keen to listen. Although the teacher has also a lot to do in education but most of it is related to the efforts of students. The student is completely responsible for the knowledge he retrieves from the teacher. The teachers while scolding student saying that "I will finish the syllabus in a day or two and my responsibility would be over". This statement clearly implies that a teacher is responsible for merely finishing up the syllabus. The extra knowledge to be extracted is the complete responsibility of student. The student has to finish up the home work given, ask doubt and question and pay attention. The students are the one who could turn a lecture into either a boring one or an interactive session. Everything was going well on the other hand suddenly it stopped due to Corona pandemic. The whole nation is shutter down. Schools, colleges, university all closed. Restaurants, hotels buses trains, flights, taxis all closed. Most government around the world have temporarily closed education institute in an attempt to contain the spread of Covid-19 pandemic. Man is locked inside the wall of their houses. Many examination where postponed or reschedule. Then when it felt that everything had become too much sitting at home and then juggling of being new work started again, because the pandemic has significantly destructed the education system. Schools and colleges in which it was prohibited to keep mobiles, now started opening classes and colleges through mobile and internet. The whole world shrunk between mobile and internet. Zoom app goggle classroom started studying in front of mobiles and laptops for many hours or children were given admission in the next year. In such process only a handful of privates schools could adopts online teaching method on the other hand government schools completely shut down for not having access to e-learning solution. Additions to missed opportunity for student learning. Education is more important than the examination. Education of morality should be given at home which can't be given in any real or virtual classroom.

3. Lecture Responsibility

In the teaching process, teachers must be able to combine cognitive and affective students. Before students begin lessons, teachers must maintain the emotions of trust by making students feel them. When something becomes this personal, it uses information about the person being served to change their response. Teachers must use data about students to change how we teach how students learn, and our institutional policies and practices. The teacher's ethical responsibility is the ability to find suitable solution to a particular situation and display consistent, achievable behavior, and live up to moral values, not just state them. Collective responsibility is a responsibility that is shared among individuals. Teachers must plan assignments to develop collaborative skills in various aspects to solve complex problem when solved alone.

"New learning dynamic environment stems from the interaction between teacher and students."

4. Students Responsibility in Higher Education:

Teachers prepare and motivate themselves to improve their knowledge and skills. The goal is to advance the quality of education opportunities to increase the quality of online learning are strongly. In this Corona crisis, a well-rounded and effective educational practice is also needed. It will develop skill that will drive their productivity health well- being and insecure the overall process of India. In formal education, teachers are there to teach you but in informal we have learnt yourself from the experiences, nature. In higher education also, we have to give feedback to our teacher, parents to improve the level of education.

1.5. Impacts of ICT in education

Information and Communication Technologies (ICT) may be a term which refers to technologies which are used for collecting, storing, editing and spending on information in various forms. A personal computer is an example of the utilization of ICT in education. Multimedia is additionally a frequently used term to ask a mixture of knowledge carriers, for instance video, CD-ROM, floppy disc and Internet and software during which the likelihood for an interactive approach is offered. ICT enable the transformation of teaching, research and learning processes in the least levels. It empowers teachers and students, making significant contributions to the education fraternity. The ICT has been organized in several courses consistent with the goal, purpose and area of applicability. What is being learned also depends on the sort of education and therefore the level of the scholars. Education prepares students for the utilization of ICT in education, future occupation and social life.

In the education sector, we've seen ICT having an enormous impact within the schools and colleges curriculum by introducing it as a area of study. For example in Universities and tertiary colleges, KCA as an example, we see ICT as a field of study in several professional disciplines. Some of the disciplines include Information Technology, computing , Software Engineering, Data Communications, Computer Engineering, Management Information Systems, Mobile Computing, among the various others. This successively has led to professions within the ICT, both in education system and therefore the industry. The ICT as an object may be a key driver on the utilization of ICT in other application areas. In most cases, ICT is employed as a tool, for instance while making assignments, collecting data and documentation, communicating and conducting research. Typically, ICT is employed independently from the topic matter. In current higher learning institutions, coursework's, assignments and other work are not any longer done the normal way of paper work. They are done and submitted electronically.

ICT has transformed the way the education is delivered. It is as a tool for teaching and learning itself, the medium through which teachers can teach and learners can learn. There are many various types during which ICT has been envisaged as a medium for teaching and learning included computer assisted learning, web-learning, computer-classes, online training, distance education, eLearning, virtual learning, digital training, etc. ICT is employed as a tool for administration and management of record like school examination preparation and printing, examination results compilation, timetable, school fee and faculty attendance.

In most primary and education sector in Kenya, the particular situation is that the majority teachers and schools don't possess sufficient ICT educational skills and equipment at the present. Although teachers consult one another more frequently, the teacher decides on the tutorial practice in his class room. He is responsible and has the chance to show within the way he pleases. However, in practice (the classical teaching situation), the pedagogies usually seems to be determinative and limits the teacher in his possibilities. Education and teacher are tied to a selected content of education, timetables, amount of face-to-face instruction, instruction time, class rooms, etc. Even the teacher's status is laid down. Legal provisions also determine the tutorial practice in schools. Because of these constraints teachers are insufficiently challenged and stimulated to make powerful learning environments and guide students in their learning processes individually and thus, the utilization of ICT does not take place.

Positive impacts of ICT in education

ICT play a task on three fundamental aspects of education: access, quality and price . It has advanced knowledge by expanding and widening access to education, by improving the standard of education and reducing its cost while extending the education to the remote areas through Virtual, E-Learning, online and distance learning. ICT in education has provided more employment opportunities within the education system directly and indirectly through academic and non-academic staff. E-Learning may be a promising tool for expanding and widening access to tertiary education. Because they relax space and time constraints, ICTs can allow new people to participate in tertiary education by increasing the pliability of participation compared to the normal face-to-face model: working students and adults, people living in remote areas (e.g. rural), non-mobile students and even foreign students could now more easily participate in education.

Online learning allows access to education to larger number of students. The constraints of the face-to-face learning experience, that is, the dimensions of the rooms and buildings and therefore the students/teacher ratio are eliminated. With ICT, a lesson are often reproduced and communicated very cheaply via different means just like the digital recording. This has widened access to tertiary education to children and too small academic workforce. E-learning has shown a promising way for improving the quality and effectiveness of tertiary education and learning. These promises are derived from different characteristics of ICTs: the pliability of the training experience to students; enhanced access to information resources for more students; potential to drive innovative and effective ways of learning and/or teaching, including learning tools and easier use of multimedia or simulation tools.

E-learning has also led to scale back the value of tertiary education, which is critical for expanding and widening its access worldwide. It presents new opportunities for college kids having difficulties with this traditional format.

Negative impacts of ICT in education

One of the main impacts of ICT in education is moral decay. These include access to inappropriate material, violation of private privacy, and being the recipient of sexual predation, pornography, harassment, stalking, or scams and dissemination of harmful or abusive material. By use of ICT, students don't learn the essential mental arithmetic skills because they believe electronic methods including calculators. With ICT, students tend to try to to much of copying and pasting rather than learning and taking their own notes. This has led to ethical issues such as plagiarism. Relying on spell check and grammar features of software's like Microsoft data processing cause lower literacy skills because they have a tendency to form the scholars think less.

Education is one of the means for developing nation and converts to developed nation in a global world with the help of information and communication tools. The word 'Internet' which is most probably started at early morning tea and continues till eyes light dark. Basically today internet is working as life partner for a large number of people in his\ her life cycle. Who fulfill their perception according to their choices? Such technology of modern era is not only help in personal basis but a large variant of professional lives. Mainly for educational purpose, it is widely used to gather information and improve the academic excellence in different fields, with the internet access in education, a wide range of ideas, teaching and learning resources techniques. New innovation and creative thoughts have been widely used and share in global platform with the help of internet.

No doubt ICT plays an important role in the field of education in every step of human being basically in teaching learning process. Students will use the different search engine like Google, Yahoo, etc. They supply a large number of information within the few seconds. Information and communication is based on the internet services. Today ICT is a powerful tool in the world which is preferred by mostly everyone. Importance of Information and Communication Technology for professional and non professional are given below:

- **Cost Effective and Affordable Education**

One of the largest barriers to education is high cost, which is not affordable for weaker section of the people living in our society. But this bridge gap between the learner and reader will fill with the help of new modern technology.

- **Direct Interaction with Sender and Receiver**

The information and communication technology allowed students to be constant touch with their classmates and guides there are many applications which help with information about bridge in between them such as messaging apps, chat apps.

- **Easy accessible through the Worldwide**

Learner can easily access the required material which is essential for academic excellence. Student's clear their doubts with the help of tutorial videos on different platforms. Teacher can record the lectures and provide it to the students for revision according to their own timetable and reading efficiency.

- **Stands with era and technology**

For a good livelihood it is necessary to update with new technology and scenario exist in our society. There is a huge amount of information available for every subject. Information and communication technology keep up every individual to update himself\herself with the latest information regarding the subject in which they want to upgrade with new innovation ideas.

1.6.ICT and it's scope:

1. World wide web (WWW) is updating the knowledge warehouses for students, teachers, researcher because of tremendous advancement of ICT. An individual from Village likewise, can allude the most recent data and exploration everyday.Open universities and distance instruction through ICT are new openings for working individuals to gain, information to learn at home too.
2. Television broadcast is one of the best communication media to educate the students, farmers, sportsman with latest information with video clips.The costly and difficult experiments, advanced surgery for medical students etc. can be viewed.

3. The curriculum information about textbooks, reference books and references are available on Internet. Even one can complete a course of foreign university by using Internet, which is very cost effective. The giants in the field of computer viz Microsoft, Oracle corporation conduct the online certificate at prometric centers at different places over the globe.

4. Audio cassettes, video tapes, audio and video CDs, video multimedia interactive CDs are available in the market for all types of students from KG(kinder garden) to PG (Post graduate) students.Even teachers can develop the content CDs using computers.

5. Instead of overhead projectors no LCD projectors can be used for effective learning for large number of students.

6. The manpower, the human mistakes can be avoided by online examination. It maintains objectivity of examination.And requires minimum time even examination can be conducted on demand Maharashtra state board is conducting online examination for Information Technology subject of XII standard. Maharashtra Knowledge Corporation (MKCL) also conduct online examination for MSCIT course and the result is declared as soon as student clicks the end exam button.

The three words Information, Communication and Technology have their own separate meaning. But, the meaning of the three words collectively, ICT is becoming a part and parcel of human being. ICT is very useful in almost all areas of human life. ICT can also be represented by a schematic diagram, as given below:

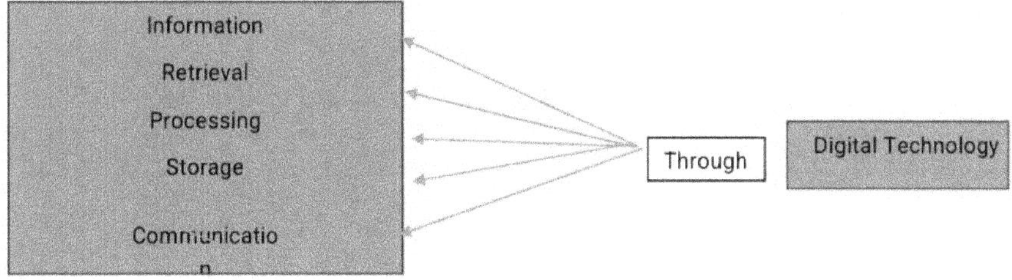

ICT tools:

Information and communication technologies (ICT) have become commonplace entities in all aspects of life. Across the past twenty years the use of ICT has commonly changed the practices and technique of basically a wide range of attempt inside business and organization. Guidance is a socially arranged development and quality tutoring has usually been connected with strong teachers having significant levels of individual contact with understudies. The usage of ICT in tutoring fits more understudy centered learning settings. Yet, with the world moving quickly into computerized media and data, the job of ICT in training is turning out to be increasingly significant and this significance will proceed to develop a lot in the 21st century. Portions of the ICT Tools which are utilized for instructing learning measure are as underneath. These apparatuses assist students with getting abilities needed for smooth correspondence. These apparatuses are useful to educators just as understudies:

<table>
<tr><td>

- ❖ Internet
- ❖ Socialmedia
- ❖ Online facilities
- ❖ Online language related courses
- ❖ Feature films
- ❖ E-creationtools

</td><td>

- ❖ Listening /speaking facilitativee-tools
- ❖ Virtual learning environments
- ❖ Computer Assisted Languagel earnin

</td></tr>
</table>

ICT tools used in education

- Mobile, Desktop and laptops
- Projector
- Digital cameras
- Desktop and laptops Projector
- Digital cameras
- Printer Photocopier

- PenDrive
- Ipods
- Ipads
- Webboards
- Scanners
- Microphones

ICT can be useful for a teacher in the following ways:

1. It is helpful in the professional development of the teachers. A teacher can learn various language skills with the help of ICT. He can do various certification programs run by the famous educational institutions like Cambridge University, British Council etc. These programs help in enhancing his capacity to teach his subject content easy, economic and more understandable.

2. A teacher can increase his domain of knowledge with the help of e-journals, e-magazines and e-library that can be achieved only through the use of ICT. He can also participate in discussions and conferences with the experts of his subject teaching to improve his knowledge and skills through audio and video conferencing.

3. ICT helps a teacher to learn innovative methods of teaching. He can work with the students on various project and assignments. It also helps him in providing teaching contents,home works etc.

4. He may take an interest in different in-administration preparing projects and workshops which are fundamental for his expert improvement with the assistance of ICT.

5. ICT encourages an instructor to direct his understudies about the learning materials accessible on web, digital books ,e-diaries ,e-magazines and social locales like connected in which are useful in better mastering of subject abilities and subject skills.

6. ICT also helps him framing curriculum of subjects. He can study curriculum of different countries to study their pros and cons,

challenges as well as sociological and psychological issues related to learners. All these things help him in framing a curriculum that leads to achieve the aims and objectives of subject of teaching.

ICT can be useful for a student in the following ways:

1. Student can study through online resources. There are different resources through which it will be helpful for students to understand topic. Students can learn from their place and at any time.
2. Students can meet teachers online and get required knowledge about the subject.
3. Students can have no limit of time and place.

In this way there are different apps through which teaching learning process is becoming more easy. These apps help teachers and students to communicate with each other and get knowledge of particular subject. Teachers are also learning different apps use for teaching and students are using for learning process. In this way ICT tools are helpful in this pandemic situation. These tools are helping teachers as well as students.

1.7. The benefits of using ICT in the present pandemic situation

Increased flexibility of time: Learning and teaching can occur at times that are more convenient and productive for both students and teachers. Students can work at their own pace within a given framework and the online learning and teaching engagement process can be broken into smaller more frequent portions of time, with an opportunity for reflection in between. Increased flexibility of location Learning and teaching can take place in any location (home, office,) and can include students and teachers from diverse geographical locations

Information sharing online education provides opportunities to access and share information more easily and readily. Teachers and students are able to join online communities of practice based on their area of interest rather than their geographic location.

Diverse and enriching experience Online education can enhance the student learning experience by providing opportunities for cross-disciplinary, cross-cultural and/or cross-campus collaborations. This learning experience can occur at a local, national or international level, and can be enriched by increased interaction and engagement, peer feedback, and group work skills.

Improvement in learning material there is a great opportunity for universities and colleges to start improving the quality of the learning material that is used in the teaching and learning process. The world of education and learning is moving towards online training. The benefits are undeniable: - reduced costs; great flexibility for the student and the ability to train thousands of people all over the globe at the same time. In addition, one can monitor what students are doing at any given moment, and it breaks with the inertia and passivity of classroom courses. However, e-learning is not without its faults. Online teaching comes with its own particular characteristics, which can jeopardize the success of the training. (game-learn.com) Body language and eye contact, which are important cues for the teacher, are difficult to perceive in an online class. Teachers don't receive a continual feedback in the form of student reaction, which is a must for the teacher to know about the effectiveness of teaching. The aspect of learning is severely limited in online education.

Finally, education is not just about developing social skills and sportsmanship among the students, which is built over the years. Relying solely on online mode may hinder the holistic development of children, and many may underperform later in their professional and personal lives. In this situation when technology based learning is the only way for continue the education again then the other hand this technology based learning is the reason for disrupted the education of many more children. Stakeholders also be not fully ready for utilize the technological device and as a pitfall of digital learning, they may be demotivated and frustrated from teaching and learning. These circumstances forced to think that there are a urgent need for restructuring our education system (Rieley,2020). So it is the time for discussing the issues and challenges of online learning in this pandemic situation.

The role of the Information and Communication Technology (ICT) has suddenly seen a significant surge due to scrupulous isolation and lockdown measures shutting down all academic institutions across the world due to coronavirus pandemic. The unprecedented, unparalleled, and challenging situations have brought the academic fraternity under insurmountable mental pressure elevating the dominance and rate of anxiety, depression, stress, and even neurological disruptions. It left with no options for teachers, students, and users but to acquire digital skills to acquaint themselves with the distinctive rise of e-learning, whereby teaching is conducted remotely and on digital platforms. Further, the development of its tools, components, and the possibilities offered by ICT are deftly used in teaching and learning, thereby, helping improve the quality of learning and teaching at all levels across disciplines globally. The sudden shift from face to face (F2F) to virtual or online teaching has brought a rise in websites to assist teachers across the world in digitalizing teaching tools. Today, we witness virtual classes, educational videos, online exams, online worksheets/ assignments submission, meetings, professional development webinars, question-answer sessions, and individual help to develop digital pedagogical resources. The digital platforms help teachers and students improve their skills and boost their credentials staying.

The whole human kingdom is being enlightened through proper and systematic education as it provides us knowledge and environment to enhance our skills to change them for the better. Education also helps us to develop our own perspective of looking at our lives, prepares us to have our own points of view and form our own opinions on different facets of life. Education today is not the process of gaining information. Any willing person can have access to immense data and information nowadays through different websites and e-based platforms. Only education can train us to interpret different issues and events in our lives. We can learn not only through the lessons in our textbooks, but from our teachers, gurus, and mentors who guide us on how to read those books. We also learn from our own lives through our practical experiences and hands-on trainings. In short, education helps us to acquire knowledge, skills, values and attitudes to make informed decisions, lead meaningful lives, and undertake active roles in contemporary society. But the unexpected covid-19 situation changed the Process of thinking. The COVID-19 pandemic has been weakling the whole earth including our country India. Therefore, all the enrolled students in schools, colleges and universities of India have been unable to go to their institutions for almost a year due to the restrictions imposed to check the spread of the novel corona virus since the middle of March 2020.This cause a large gaps between the students and their students including their teachers and mentors.

Since there were no clear policy and guidelines in most of the higher institutions on online teaching, several questions such as what to teach, how to teach, what should be the duties of the teacher and the student, the workload of the teacher, the teaching environment, and the implications for education equity, etc., were not clear. Problems such as the infrastructure, teachers' and students' experience on online teaching. The challenge related to COVID-19 is assessing students remotely. In higher institution, assessment has three major purposes: to support learning, to execute accountability, and to provide certification and progress.

CHAPTER TWO

ONLINE EDUCATION

The 'COVID -19' pandemic has sparked a global realization that our current way of life does not work normally. One such critical area where the need for charge has become evident is education. The effects of the Novel Corona Virus' and there by its preventive measures, has up ended the life of students, parents and teachers. Any kind of pandemic faces the world a new kind of global crises and challenges. It affects almost every part of our life. If we look into our past decades then we can find that globally we faced so many pandemic situations and every pandemic situations faced a terror situation equally almost every part of this world. We can also find that every pandemic situation changed the way of normal education. These changes have certainly caused a degree of inconvenience, but this also promoted new examples of education innovation. The recent 'Novel Corona Virus' has also changed the normal way of education. Although it is too early to judge how reactions to 'Novel Corona Virus' will affect the education system around the world, there are signs suggesting that it could have a long lasting impact on the trajectory of learning innovation and digitization.

2.1. Problem and Challenges of online teaching learning process

- **Misconception about the internet and its usefulness**

Basically in developing countries, people can use the internet site for social networking and inoperative sense work. So the large number of people believed that if you promote the digital gadgets it can be used for negative purposes.

- **Connectivity**

Most of students, teachers and educator say that, it is the speed of the connection that is the major bottleneck. Connectivity also affects where the students access the internet. Students without internet can't connect with teachers or classmates. Information idea can be shared only with high speed network.

- **Language problem or localization of content**

Basically in our country three language formula is working, among in which, the other language is more preferred. An unfortunately large number of language material or contents are available in English languages. Because the English language is supposed to be the universal language. The program is running in English which is not the studies native tongue. As a result lots of students are bore from studies. Language makes the international boundary between learner and information provider.

- **Infrastructure of Social Education System**

Huge laws of infrastructure in school and our educational system. Learner are incapable to use the modern and advanced technology, basically in rural parts of India, They are unable to operate and hard to get the online education system in their lifestyle.

- **Attitudes of parents towards E-learning-**

Most of educated or literally educated families and parents don't have positive attitudes towards E-learning. Parents thought that, their child uses the internet as a social media for chatting and socializing, watching movies and listening to music. This simply wastes of time or delays on school work submission. As a result poor academic result. Parents believed that school dodging was reported among affects associated with the internet used among secondary school.

- **Lack of speed of Web Band**

Despite the large number of internet users in developing country like India. The still level of the network used in rural area is 2g, 3g network. Infrastructure speed of the internet is too low level; we can fail to think about the online classes.

- **Lack of motivation towards the modern technology**

The internet penetration level stood at just 40% to 42% in India, which is less than half of the total population. People are unable to easily accept the modern technology due to safety norms and negative advertisement. Both central and state governments don't provide the sufficient aid to promote the importance of modern technology in a global world.

- **Inefficiency of Teachers and Teacher Educator**

Still now around 40% of our teacher and teacher educator are incapable to use the modern gadgets and technology, which is necessary to operate the online classes and discussion. The teachers and teacher educator have lack of confused as what to teach and how to teach with the help of modern technology and application and lack of literacy about the computer and modern advance apps.

- **Access issue**

There are roughly 5.5 million households with school age children, who don't have broadband internet access at home. This means millions of students are being left behind the service. The infrastructure problem concerns those living in rural areas, where the internet is available with bandwidth problems.

2.2. Present Scenario of Education System in Pandemic Scenario

As discussed above, like the other sectors, any kind of pandemic largely affects the education sectors. The corona pandemic has made a global impact and hits most of the sectors, with education being one of the most affected ones. Students across the world are losing valuable time in their education during the imposed lockdown amidst fears of pandemic. The situation has forced the schools to shut down and the students to stay at home. No wonder, the children as well as parents feel emotionally and psychologically drained at this juncture. According to the UNESCO's Global Education Monitoring Report as of March 28, 2020, the 'COVID-19' pandemic is causing more than 1.6 billion children and youth to be out of school in 161 countries. This is close to 80% of the world's enrolled students. We were already experiencing the global learning crises, as many students were in schools but were not learning the fundamental skills needed for life. What should we be worried about in this phase of the crises that might have an immediate impact on children and youth? (1)Losses in learning (2) Increased drop-out rates (3) Children missing their most important meal of the day. Moreover, most countries have very unequal education systems, and these negative impacts will be felt disproportionately by the poor children. Most schools and institutions have come up with the idea of online classes for students to continue their respective academic years, instead of wasting time due to the delay in reopening of educational institutions.

2.3. Emergency E-Learning and the Securitization of face-to-face classes

The 'COVID- 19' response is not the first time that emergency e-learning programs have been considered as appropriate crises-response measures. A similar strategy was observed in 2009, where 67% of 'H1N1' contingency plans involved substitution of online classes for face to face classes. In response to institutions closures, UNSESCO recommended the use of distance learning programs and open educational applications and platforms that institutions and teachers can use to reach learners remotely and limit the disruptions of education. This is not the first time a pandemic has forced distance learning upon unprepared students. In 1665, 'The Great Plague' of London forced Sir Isaac Newton and his classmates out of Trinity College for a year. Still Newton used his time at home to develop his early work on calculus using prisms to develop his theories on optics, and making his famous gravity observations.

All kinds of educational institutions have to be shut to prevent the spread of the virus and as an alternative of face to face education. This has given a way to online education. E-learning or online learning platforms provide anywhere, anytime easy access for smoothly continuing the teaching-learning process. E-learning programs are clutching the moment and trying to plug the academic void created by the closure of educational establishments due to Corona Virus pandemic. E-learning signifies the method of sharing and communicating knowledge via multimedia platforms.

As lockdown continue throughout the world, many individuals are heading online for help such as the 1.3 million people signed up for 'The science of well being,' a free course from Yale University. Since the end of

2019, its enrollment numbers have raised up 295%, and in March 2020 more than half a million new learners signed up within a matter of weeks. The online enrollment boom is being experienced elsewhere, too. A course that also looks at the science of happiness, run by the University of California, Berkeley, has crossed its own registration record by drawing half a million learners globally .

The Corona Virus pandemic and the ensuing lockdown has forced the schools, colleges and the universities across India to temporarily shut and this virus had created a big gap in the education system despite the central and state Governments doing their best to provide support for e-learning and online education. NASSCOM, a trade association of Indian Information Technology association of India is offering courses such as artificial intelligence Foundation Course, AI for everyone, and other similar subjects for free or its portal skill up online, which was launched with support from Ministry of Electronics and information technology (Meity), India. 'Tata consultancy service' (TCS), an Indian multinational technology (IT) service and consulting company is offering a 15 day digital certification program called 'Career Edge Knockdown the Lock down' for free through the corona virus TCS, ION. Due to this corona virus pandemic many online learning platforms are offering free access to their service, including platforms like 'BYJUS', a Bangalore (India) based educational technology and online tutoring firm, since announcing free live classes, BYJU's has seen a 200% increase in the number of new students using its product, according to Mrinal Mohit, the company's chief operating officer. According to a latest report, the Indian e-learning market size was USD247 million, comprising 1.6 million users in 2016. Due to the corona virus pandemic it is expected witness an 8x growth to reach USD 1.96 billion and the current user base will grow at 44 percent CAGR to 9.6 million users by 2021.

There are, however, challenges to overcome. Some students without reliable internet access and technology struggle to participate in digital learning; this gap is seen across countries and between income brackets within countries. For example, whilst 95% of students in Switzerland, Norway, and Australia have a computer to use for their school work, only 35% in Indonesia do, according to OECD data.

In the US, there is a significant gap between those from privileged and disadvantaged backgrounds: whilst virtually all 15 year old from a privileged background said they had a computer to work on, nearly 25% of those from disadvantaged backgrounds did not. While some school and governments have been providing digital equipment to students in need, such as in New South Wales, Australia, many are still concerned that the pandemic will widen the digital divide.

2.4. Advantages of Online Education during a Pandemic Situation

As we have discussed earlier that a pandemic situation may greatly affects the normal face-to -face education system and may close the all kinds of educational institutions, so e-learning may be the ultimate substitution for smoothly continuing the teaching-learning processes. Below there is discussed the major benefits of Online Education or e-learning during a pandemic situation:

(a) Engagement: As a pandemic scenario may close all types of face to face educational institutions, so e-learning may engage the students and teachers in normal teaching learning process. The students-teachers can smoothly continuing their teaching-learning process through any kind of web based or satellite based devices.

(b)Minimized the chance of virus affected: As face- to- face teaching-learning process does no maintain the social distancing, so in a pandemic situation it is very risk or not possible to continuing the face- to- face teaching-learning. Therefore in a pandemic scenario it is one of the precaution first priorities to shut the all types of face- to- face teaching-learning classes. In this situation e-learning may be the better substitution for the teaching-learning process. It minimized the chance of virus affected to the students as well as the teachers and also the persons related to the face- to- face classes. Online education provides a safe and effective alternative to the face- to- face classroom.

(c)Uninterrupted teaching-learning process: Another advantage of e-learning or online classes is that it may provide the uninterrupted teaching-learning process. As in a pandemic situation, it may close or shutdown all kinds of face-to-face educational institutions, so as a substitution e-learning or online education provide an uninterrupted teaching-learning process.

(d)Social distancing can be exercised: Amidst the regulations of social distancing and self isolation, the students if allowed to attend schools may not be able to exercise of safety precautions in an effective manner. It would be very tough to control the students from playing or touching each other which might make the situation of virus spread out of control. Online classes or e-education in the comfort of their future and also in controlling the virus spread.

(e)Motivate the learners: As an alternative of face-to-face learning, online learning may be the best alternative learning method in this regard. It is felt that students are actually more responsive and active in online classes, compared to when they are in physically presents in a traditional class rooms. This could be because this is a new concept and they are excited to explore it with the teachers. They also don't get distracted by their classmates, which is frequently happens in a face- to- face traditional class. So considering the students' motivation in learning in a pandemic situation online learning may be the best alternative learning method of traditional learning methods.

2.5 Disadvantages of Online Education during a Pandemic Situation

Online learning may be the better substitute of face to face or class room learning, but it will be never be the replacement of face to face of class room lessons. It has some demerits too.

(a) Lack of developing values: Accepting the benefits of e-learning method doesn't mean rejecting the traditional class room pedagogy. The convenience and low cast model of e-learning cannot replace the experiential learning of human values and character development of the class room setting. Education is not limited to the syllabus only; it also includes discipline, manners, morals and interaction with other students and teachers. These types of values are difficult to inject through online teaching.

(b)Lack of attention: Class rooms are important as the children sit together and concentrate on a particular topic. They are able to learn new skills in such an environment and teachers and students have their full attention to each other, which may not be found in an e-learning or virtual class room platform.

(c) Affects the evaluation process: In teaching-learning process students evaluation or examination is another important part of academic calendar, but sometimes evaluation or test is not possible to evaluate the students' academic achievement. So still now in some way virtual evaluation is not the appropriate alternative of traditional examination or test.

(d) Unequal accesses to technology: It is an unequal and discrimination to those of the rural or remote areas and to the disadvantaged families where the lack of accessibility of technology or fast and reliable internet facility has been seen. Many students have not been able to take the advantages of the virtual platform because they do not have a suitable device at home or lack of a good internet connection. In remote areas, many parents don't own Android phones or gadgets, which is a harsh reality. Also there are some who have these gadgets but are unable to pay the price of the data. Sometimes, the signal is lost and the class is missed. As a result, a sudden shift to online learning during a pandemic is bound to worsen the learning gap for low income households, poor districts, and poorer countries.

(e) Creates physical and mental Problem: During an online class, too much screen time can be perilous for health. Prolonged online sessions can be overwhelming and may lead to problems related to vision, body posture and sleep disorder both to the teachers and students.

(f) Lack of technological literacy: To access the online learning, both the students and facilitators must possess a minimum level of technological knowledge in order to function successfully in a suitable environment. For example, they must be able to use a variety of search engines and be comfortable navigating on the World Wide Web (www) as well as familiar with Newsgroups, FTP procedures and e-mail. It can undoubtedly say that these kinds of illiteracy have largely been seen in both the students and the facilitators worldwide.

(g) Lack of safety and security: User friendly and reliable technology is critical to a successful online program. However, even the most sophisticated technology is not fully safe and reliable. There are so many numbers of illegal activities and security threats taking place on the internet. Consequently, the e-learning environment is inevitably exposed to constant security threats, risks and attacks. Many educational institutions and students rush into adopting e-learning without fully understanding the related security concerns.

(h) Lack of practical experience: Learning with doing is the best method for the students to achieve the educational experiences. Practical assignments are often carried out in group and pair of students. These group works or pair works help to inculcate social values and values like sharing, co-operation, team spirit, compassion etc. Some skill based subjects like 'Beauty & Wellness', 'Design Thinking' , 'Handicrafts', 'Mass Media' 'Physical Education' etc. and the laboratory based subjects like 'Physics', 'Chemistry', 'Zoology', 'Botany' etc. need more important practical classes than theoretical classes. But it is sometimes very difficult or impossible to take practical and hand on experience through the online learning or virtual classes.

When the educational institutions closed at the beginning of the pandemic, not many reckoned it would change the face of education. From no Smartphone allowed in the classes, to learning only with such devices at home, it had been a massive changes that everyone involved-teachers, students and parents- is still getting accustomed to. Many institutions have begun online classed, which are still continuing. For the teacher, the move from physical classroom of 40-odd boisterous students to a room in their homes, from where they hope to impart the dame level of learning to the young ones, has been fraught with challenges and quite the learning experience.

COVID-19, Pandemic stopped every unit of life whether it's a government or a private one. Everybody gets locked under their roof and their daily routine gets disturbed. 90 % of world's Students are under the threat of Corona-virus and are the biggest sufferers who are facing a tough time, as some aspires to be future I.A.S, I.P.S and some who were preparing for various competitive exams also faced multiple challenges. Their future is at stake. Their coaching gets affected and some are short of study materials (Times of India). Talking about the weaker section which are deprived of many things due to lockdown as some families faces financial crisis, students who cannot afford advanced mobile phones and other gadgets, which are the basic necessity to learn as online classes is the only option for the various learning institutions, They are facing a jolt. Every individual is not at a par in terms of financial support and it's a need of hour to talk about those who are at the target of poverty. There are many areas which are shunned and shattered because of this turmoil COVID-19.Undoubtedly the government is looking at every aspect and came up with different plans and options to cope up with the academic loss like revised academic calendar, online classes, etc. but still, there are many areas where they need to work hard.

It has become appallingly obvious that our technology has exceeded our humanity. Today we live in the so called ultra-modern age where technology has revolutionized our world and daily lives. Technology has created amazing tools and resources, putting useful information at our fingertips. But the crisis of COVID 19 has brought every sphere of life in this hi-tech century at a standstill including education. We are busy looking for answers to our future but are helpless in front of the problem of imparting education because of this virus. With time, everything around has changed, may it be technology or our way of living our lives, then why can't we find other alternatives to our age-old conventional method of imparting education through physical presence of a teacher and students in a classroom. The purpose of education is to enrich the mind of students but can this purpose be fulfilled only if education is confined within four walls?

Although COVID 19 has posed an important question in front of us, i.e. how will we impart education during these difficult times and circumstances, but as they say " necessity is the mother of invention" it has also given us the rare opportunity to find new and more innovative techniques to disseminate education. This pandemic has forced more than 1.2 million students out of their classrooms and has brought imparting of knowledge at a halt. There are only two solutions to this problem today, either we completely leave this teaching and learning process till this crisis can be controlled, but that isn't a viable option or we need to find new an innovative methods of teaching without the need for classrooms so that we can stay safe as well as keep the cycle going. Virtual education in its most simple definition means that anyone who wants to lean can learn from any place in the world even if the teacher is in some other corner of the world. This medium of imparting education was earlier seen as an option for students who could not physically go to the class due to any reason. But today in a time when it is not possible for anyone of us to go to a classroom then why this alternative can't be put into practice. Both the students and the teacher can from the comfort and safety of their homes teach and learn without any burden.

With constant evolution we do not even wear the same cloths that were trending fifty years ago, or do not even prefer using the same gadgets that we used less than ten years ago. We have always lived with the notion that we will find the answers to the questions of our present in our future but in order to find a solution to this problem we do not need to wait to step into the future, the answer lies in our past. The longest epic in the world- The Mahabharata tells the tale of a very talented and underrated character Eklavya, a forest prince who wanted the learn the skill of archery from the great Guru Drona but couldn't do so because Guru Drona was the Kul Guru of Hasthinapur and teaching Eklavya was be treason for him. But Eklavya's dedication to learn was far stronger than Dronacharya's will for not teaching. The young boy built a statue of Guru Drona in his hut and would stealthily observe the guru teaching his pupils and then would come back and practice the same art. The boy's determination was so strong that soon he outperformed Dronacharya's most cherished and prized pupil

Arjun. If a boy starting from scratch with almost no resources could match the skill of the best archer in the world then how is that people like us who have the entire world at our finger tips have such limited reach.

This would not only benefit the education system but also in the environment, with the entire process of education taking place virtually there would be no need left for maintaining so many textbooks and notebooks. Tests and assignments can be conducted online where students can instantly know their performance too. A lot of people may feel that this mode of studying is nothing more but a cheap substitute of actual classroom learning and that no matter what the quality of learning on this platform will never match that of physically learning in schools and colleges. Even if assessments and assignments are conducted online there would never be 100% transparency in the process and there someone will always bypass the system. Such people need to understand that this tool of virtual education is like a surgery scalpel if used wisely can save someone's life but if used with the wrong intention then is no less than a knife for taking someone's life. Even if a teacher does everything possible at their end, as students it is their responsibility to take the matter at hand seriously because the teacher at the other end will not be at profit, it is the students who need to make the most out of this opportunity and diligently work, not towards finding and exploiting the loopholes of the system but towards fixing these loopholes. This age old system of education has proved to be the only solution to the pandemic crisis.

The nationwide lockdown due to the spread of Covid-19 has brought about a paradigm shift in the mode of dissemination of knowledge. There is sprout of on-line classes in this pandemic period to meet the educational needs of students. Use of digital platform in learning is quite obvious in a situation like this. Universities, schools, colleges have switched towards e-learning to continue the uninterrupted flow of knowledge despite the rising number of Corona virus cases in various parts of the country. In this fight against the pandemic what cannot suffer is education and knowledge dissemination. The various modes of knowledge dissemination adopted are ZOOM, WEBEX, Google Classroom, Microsoft team, FB live etc. The discussion around adopting digital technologies for educational purposes has now turned into a reality, owing to the Corona breakdown throughout the world. Virtual classrooms and online tools used on this digital platform allow the academicians/school staff to develop engagement between the teachers and students as close as in a classroom environment. These tools can also aid in organizing teachers and parent meetings, staff/management meetings and can save both time and cost while providing the necessary interactivity.

A virtual classroom is a digital replica of a traditional classroom or training room. The instructors teach, and the participants learn in real-time, face-to-face but via internet-enabled technology devices. The classroom or the meeting room staple-whiteboard-remains intact. Brainstorming, ideation, and discussions happen in real-time. Tests are given and taken pre and post the session. The reports are ready right after the session is over.

A virtual classroom enables students to access quality teachers anywhere on the planet as long as they both have a reliable internet connection. This does pose a problem for students who due to any reason may not have good internet connectivity during the duration of the class, but thanks to this medium a teacher can record their lectures and later students can access these lectures as per their convenience. The students can note down any queries and can clarify the doubts later. This can break down most of the common barriers to synchronous learning: cost, distance and timing.

Everything remains the way it is. The only difference is that an online classroom uses technology to support instruction and learning. George Couros has rightly said that "technology will never replace great teachers, but in the hands of great teachers, it's transformational". Virtual education is the perfect blend of teachers and technology coming together and in order to provide a gateway for young minds to indulge in learning despite the lockdown which keeps them productive and helps them not loose connect with the subjects.

While the students are restricted to stay indoors and cannot go to school, schools can come to them through digital platform. Colleges and universities across the world are getting creative with online options to keep students safe and healthy at home. Virtual classrooms are the classrooms functioning in a system of virtual reality. These are in fact, the cyber classrooms where the teacher and the students can converse in real time. The virtual classrooms are capable of replacing partially or totally the conventional educational, evaluative and administrative functioning of a regular classroom by adopting advanced computer and ICT technologies like the Internet, e-mail, on line chatting, video conferencing, ZOOM, Google Classroom, Microsoft Team etc. These are a number of options available to the students for interacting with their teachers as permitted by the organizational system of a virtual classroom or campus. The teachers may also make use of these interaction opportunities for seeking active participation of the students in the instructional process, asking questions for testing their comprehension and evaluate their progress besides giving them freedom for removing their doubts and quenching their thrust for knowledge.

Virtual classroom system may also evolve its own system for assigning practice work, projects, and questions for reinforcing, fixing and evaluating the progress of the students. It can upload the needed material on its website for this purpose at regular intervals and the students may be asked to do the desired work and send it back for needed checking, feedback, guidance and evaluation on the part of the teachers.

Virtual classrooms have some unique advantages of providing two dimensional benefits to the learners- one comprising of the time and space relaxed opportunities of learning and the other involving classroom encounters in their proper virtual reality. It has provided a great amount of flexibility to the learners in getting the desired learning experiences. The facilities regarding receiving instructions or gaining learning experiences are available during 24 hours of all the 7 weekdays. It cannot be imagined in any other system of regular classroom set up and hence quite capable of allowing the learners better utilize their leisure hours without hampering their day-to-day routines.Instructions can be delivered to a geographically dispersed audience at one time. Today various webinars are being conducted on these online platforms through which the instructors and learners get the rich experience of collaborating with other learners and instructors from around the world. The attendance is automatically tracked. Moreover, online collaboration typically incorporates more communication tools such as chat, open discussion boards, polls and different multimedia content.

Although teaching and learning in a virtual classroom provide an experience similar to the physical one, it requires new pedagogical approaches and a redesign of the instructional model that includes the following characteristics:

- Teacher student interaction: teaching-learning in virtual classroom can only be successful with the active participation and engagement of the learners. During the virtual session there should be opportunities for frequent interaction between the teacher and the students using variety of activities such as brainstorming, small group discussion, collaborative and individual tasks, question and answer sessions, hands-on experience, etc. This creates a positive learning environment and helps the learners achieve the expected outcomes.

- Student centered instruction: Virtual classroom requires student centered instruction which moves students from passive receivers of information to active participants in their own discovery process. The teacher needs to create opportunities for both independent learning and learning from one another, and guide the learners in developing and practicing the skills they need. This increases the motivation level of the learners, as well as their interest in the learning activities.

- Emotionally protected environment: Interactions in a virtual classroom create the sense of a more informal and safer emotional environment as the learners can participate from any place of their comfort. The learning process is much more focused because the student is at liberty of arranging his surroundings in a way that leads to minimum or zero distraction. Psychologically safe environment leads to better learning outcomes. It also fosters creativity, confidence, and a willingness to experiment on the part of the learners. The virtual teacher also has a crucial role here – they need to foster a safe forum which does not lack mutual respect and ensure equal opportunities to participate, and the free sharing of different viewpoints. The teacher can enhance the intellectual ability of the learners and make things more personalized by adding options for self-directed learning, as well as by communicating more frequently with every student through a Learning Management System.

- Variety of Content Presentation and Learning Activities: Presenting the content through various types of media like text, images, diagrams, audio, video, etc. retains the attention and interest of the learners. When a teacher uses various sources to present the content, it greatly improve the learning process by providing a flexible learning experience which caters the various needs and preferences of the students.

- Positive feedback: Virtual classroom allows for immediate feedback from both the teacher and the students in both a specific and a general way. Feedback is an essential part of effective learning. It helps students understand the subject being taught and gives them clear guidance on how to improve their learning. Feedback can improve a student's confidence, self-awareness and enthusiasm for learning.

Virtual classroom system in spite of its so many advantages and virtues is found to suffer from a number of loopholes and limitations. The flexibility of virtual classroom to the learners for taking their studies at their will, convenience, comfort and adjustment of the space and timings according to their needs may by misutilized on the part of the students especially when they are younger in age and are not matured enough to shoulder their responsibilities for the building of their career or are lazy by nature.

A virtual classroom cannot be turned into real classroom in total. Real time face to face interactive experiences are not provided in the virtual classroom. The warmth of the teacher-pupil relationship, the charms of the group cohesion and fellowship etc. prevailed in the social and emotional climate of the conventional classrooms are altogether absent in the virtual classroom system.

Along with the curricular instruction work, the organization of co-curricular activities, student welfare services, community activities, the interaction with the parents and the members of the community etc. help the conventional system much in seeking the all round balanced development of the personality of the children, the sole aim of education. However, such things are completely lacking in a system of virtual classroom. Therefore, in the absence of the needed humanistic touch, socio-cultural environment and activities to promote social and moral values and opportunities for building physical, social and emotional competencies, the system of virtual classroom is quite incapable of turning our youngsters into perfect human being sensitive to moral values and mutual brotherhood.

It's the teacher that makes the difference, not the classroom. Despite its shortcomings and limitations, virtual learning can solve a number of problems coming in the way of fulfilling our constitutional obligation and duty towards our younger generation i.e. providing "education to all" and ensuring that the quality of this education is in no manner inferior to the learning that takes place inside classrooms. Quality education is our only hope in order to help lift our country from the debris of this pandemic.

Even before the lockdown was enforced in the 3rd week of March, 2020, the state governments in their individual capacities declared the schools and colleges and the other educational institutions closed for a certain period of time from the middle of March. The closure was extended for some more time and finally the lockdown was declared. Thus the education system has been hampered for the last one and a half months. This is about regular classes in the educational institutions. Just before the full lockdown, international flights were banned from leaving and entering the country, thereby restricting people from going abroad to attend scheduled international seminars, workshops and also from visiting foreign universities for taking and giving classes and lectures etc. This was followed by cancellation of the national and domestic flights also thus resulting into people not being able to visit the places for educational purpose even inside the country. Finally with the lockdown, the trains also stopped running and thus the scheduled seminars etc had to be cancelled in all the stages, like, national, state and regional, and even local. Not only have seminars been cancelled, even visiting educational institutes for other purposes had to be postponed, for example, taking viva for thesis, projects etc and for other administrative purposes.

With the full lockdown being imposed in the country, the education sector initially came to a standstill. This is an unprecedented and unfamiliar situation, and nobody still knows when the situation will be normal. It is imperative that the lifting of lockdown should obviously not take place in one go, but gradually, as otherwise the very purpose of the imposition of lockdown will be defeated with the spreading of the disease again. It is also true that unless the social distancing measures are removed, bringing back normalcy will be difficult. It is a known fact that the educational institutions are most vulnerable for the spread of the disease due to the mass gathering in the classrooms. Therefore unless, the infection is totally eradicated from the states, it is difficult to bring back the students to the schools, colleges, universities and other educational institutions. Resuming normal classes in classrooms therefore seems a distant dream at this time.

Gradually the system is getting accustomed to the situation. Distance classes, using various online platforms, have been started in many institutions. It is, however, difficult to say at this moment, how far it has been successful, especially when one is situated in urban areas and has the advantage of teaching an elite class.

The situation is very different when one looks at rural colleges and universities. Many students in rural areas may not have access to smartphones or computers. Even if they do, the net connectivity may not be as high as in urban areas. In any case, many students of the most elite institutions, the IITs, are not able to have access to online classes from their homes due to these reasons. Therefore some if not all of the universities, and some of the colleges have started online classes. The same can be said about other higher educational institutions, be they governmental, government-aided or autonomous. Private institutions normally draw students from affluent urban classes, and hence do not face problems in dealing with this unprecedented situation. Examinations have either been postponed or cancelled. While it is true that online examinations are not possible at this time given the existing infrastructure in the country, already canceling the exams kills the impetus of learning. The authorities could have waited for the lockdown to end before announcing such a drastic decision. India is a vast country with many complexities. The economic divide, the rural-urban divide and the resulting digital divide all have played an important role. The overall response of the country to the pandemic has thus been very mixed in the education sector.

2.6. The Future of Education

Though the coronavirus entered India in the month of January, it was not until March that the seriousness of the situation was felt. For one and a half months now the education system has been in the doldrums. In the meantime the severe economic effects of the lockdown have begun to be felt and there have been consequent social changes. No one knows at present, what the ultimate effect of this economic harshness will be once the lockdown is over. The threat looms large particularly over low-income families. Many students belonging to low income families may not be in a position to continue with their education due to a loss of income, especially those in the informal and unorganized sectors. This may especially be true for science and other technical education. At the same time, guest teachers and adhoc or Para-teachers in private educational institutes may lose their jobs as well.

So far not much political change has been seen as a result of the pandemic. Social changes may emerge due to people staying at homes day after day, forced to spend time within small families and in limited space. The strain induced by the lockdown could have long-term effects, but how this will affect the higher education system is hard to predict right now. There is some evidence that domestic violence has increased, and there may be some effects on students' education, especially if families break-up as a result of the lockdown. In any case, the resulting economic changes are sure to affect the higher education system indirectly.

2.6. Role of Technology

Technology ought not to play a bigger role in teaching of economics in the post-corona period. It has already been mentioned how the digital divide plays an important role; therefore in order to reach all students, classroom teaching is the best option. This is especially true for laboratory-based subjects. While humanities related subjects may be taught online, the teaching will not reach all students. (Lab-based practical classes cannot be held online as it is not possible to set up labs at homes, but that is another story.) My subject, economics, has aspects of both humanities and science, requiring both lectures as well as (computer-based) practical work. The practical part of the course is difficult to conduct online since all students may not own computers and in addition, we need proprietary software etc. For courses with mathematics it is difficult to give instruction online as well.

Online classes are not capable of substituting classroom lectures. The former is very seldom able to generate the interaction that is needed in a class. Moreover, the teachers' body language, which is a part and parcel of the classroom lectures and is imperative for their success, is also missing in online classes. The use of technology will not only lead to more discrimination, but also will create some practical problems. It will also lack the desired interaction in the class.

2.7. Impact of Online Education

While it is difficult to gauge the impact of the online classes in the institution so early, students of all subjects do not have the access to online connectivity, especially those staying in the rural areas. The practical classes in the lab-based subjects are also not being held online and mathematical papers are difficult to be instructed online. Hence, it can be said that the impact has not been very positive.

2.7. Effects on Research

Research has been affected in a negative way. While it is true that non-lab based research can be carried on through the students' perseverance and the contact with the mentor through telephone calls or emails, but one-to-one correspondence, with face to face discussion has no substitute. In many cases, where secondary data are needed, the students cannot visit the sources like the institution itself, offices and libraries, as all data are not available online. Similarly, primary data collection has also stopped since visiting sources is forbidden, and hence research is severely hampered. Mentorship improves only when there is face-to-face correspondence. In the lab-based subjects, research is totally stalled. Doctoral research has been hindered, both in primary and advanced stages.

Similarly, M.Phil research has also slowed down. This is a cause for concern since M.Phil is a time bound project. There is a negative effect on project work as well. Thus on the whole there has been an adverse effect on research at all the levels due to the coronavirus and COVID-19 pandemic, and the resulting lockdown effect on the economy.

Online learning offers tremendous upsides but also requires tremendous infrastructure, design and instructional requirements. It may be for now that countries post content and resources online as part of radio or TV-based instruction (or as stand-alone learning) but this "putting content online" and hoping students will learn on their own should not be a medium or long-term strategy.Since March 22, when Prime Minister Narendra Modi declared a nationwide lockdown, India has been witnessing its first break in normalcy in year's altogether. While this lockdown has forced us all to stay indoors, it has also negatively impacted the global economy, which might go further down the hill due to joblessness, pay cuts and lack of available resources.As schools and colleges are shut, education has shifted from the four walls of a classroom to phone and laptop screens. On the face of it, it has helped institutions to continue with the curriculum even during the lockdown. But online education has also brought to light the widening gaps between class and caste – as many students don't have access to e-resources (computers, laptops, internet connectivity) to be able to attend classes from home. More so, some students don't have a healthy environment at home which further causes a hindrance.

2.8. Rigidity in an Indian Education System

Our education system is primarily focused on exams and results and this is the reason why some colleges have proposed to conduct online examination, even during a lockdown. While e-education is a privilege for the students from upper and middle class, it has proved to be a nuisance for students from lower middle and working class. Regardless, our society and educational institutions continue to focus on grades, and not value-based education – which teaches students a sense of accountability and gratitude towards one and all. We need to teach students how to maintain basic hygiene in schools.

More than that, schools should teach students to be empathetic, to see their classmates as humans and as equals to themselves. During lockdown, we have come across various news reports on discriminatory behaviour against the Northeast Indians; on landlords and neighbours allegedly asking doctors, health workers, and airline staff members to leave their homes; on people violating lockdown rules to buy alcohol and so on. These instances show why we need to seriously focus on making education accessible and available to all. We need to take lessons from education systems in Japan and South Korea and teach our children to be responsible to one and others, to be humble, logical and resilient. There is a need to teach them how, as a country we have to stand together regardless of all the divisive borders and only then can we look forward to a pattern of holistic growth of our children.

2.9. Post the Lockdown, strict Protocols for Institutions to follow

1. Apart from the increased stress on health and hygiene for the safety of students and faculty, institutions will also have guidelines in place for re-opening and day-to-day operations. Physical distancing will be practised not only during classes but also during commutes in buses.
2. Special care to be taken to ensure physical distancing in buses, classes and during breaks. [Distancing markers] and 'dos and don'ts posters will be placed in every corridor to remind children how to conduct themselves in the college premises.
3. Institutions will have to fundamentally transform their operations to deliver learning outcomes while minimising the risk of COVID-19 transmission. This will require administrators to completely re-imagine their annual calendars, timetables, academic solutions and teaching methods.
4. From staggered lunch breaks to asking younger students to eat lunch in their classrooms under the supervision of the teacher, from disinfecting buses before every shift to ensuring that the middle seat is kept vacant, there will be a lot of challenges related to planning and execution. Institutions will even have to cut down the number of games and physical activity classes per week.
5. The strategy should be to have college on alternate days or double shifts to maintain physical distancing and reduce operational cost. Start the academic year by June-end online, or increase the academic year duration to avoid learning loss during the year. Maintain a distance of six feet in seating by having one student per desk, or two per medium desk, or three per long desk, with one empty seat between each student.
6. Experts also say that while all students and staff members will have to wear masks while on premises, colleges should ideally also have tie-ups with a local hospital or nursing home to have a medical professional available on call.

2.10. Changes required in the Classroom: A major change will be seen in the seating arrangements in classrooms. With physical distancing here to stay, colleges are working on tweaking their classroom furniture, its placement and making classrooms less crammed.

- Putting 30 to 40 students in a class won't be possible any longer—class sizes will need to be halved, perhaps via an alternate roster system for students. Double-seater desks are a thing of the past, as is the traditional system of tight rows of students sitting one behind another. Some suggest that there will now be 'U-shaped' classroom layouts, with gaps of at least four feet between students.
- Post COVID-19, collaborative furniture and flexi classrooms will be in. The less rigid the furniture, the better. Modular, lightweight furniture that can be used to rearrange classrooms quickly is the answer.
- When institutions reopen, teachers will not only play the role of educators but they will also be expected to mentor and counsel students. Changes in college timings and further division of classes into different sections will be a key feature as there will be an emergence of hybrid institutions.
- Home schooling would also be a new addition to the curriculum as parents who don't wish to send their children to institutions will be given access to online classes. Institutions can operate on the basis of odd-even for children. The syllabus will be reduced and blended learning will be added.

- Online and classroom education will be imparted simultaneously as there are chances that some of the parents will not send their children to institutions because of safety concerns. It would be advised to parents that they drop their children on their own vehicles. Otherwise they would have to ensure that the van conductor would take no more than three children at a time.
- The closure of physical learning spaces institution has given impetus to the movement of taking learning out of the confines of the classroom. While technology is seen as the solution to address the loss in learning time, students need a balanced blend of learning sessions with teachers and they will also need to learn how to 'self learn'.
- Blended learning and virtual classrooms would certainly be the 'new normal' for teaching and learning. Blended learning increases learners'

engagement and motivation and enables self-paced learning. The student becomes an active learner. Due to this, there would be less 'college-time' for students as they would look to invest their time in developing micro-skills and self-development with courses available online. The main takeaway from this situation would be the integration of technology in curriculum delivery.

- Institutions will need to adopt an integrated online-offline strategy, and this will require technology upgrades in most Indian institutions. Teachers, on the other hand, will need to become adept at using technology while also ensuring that there is personalisation of instructions to each student. With an integrated online-offline strategy, institutions will be able to manage alternate-day schooling seamlessly. It is prudent for institutions to run on alternate days with tasks clearly demarcated for at-college days (offline learning) and at-home days (online learning)."

- Institutions do much more than teaching children how to read and write. They also provide nutrition, health and hygiene services and mental and psychological support for children. In the post-Covid era, each college system needs to evaluate its health and safety measures in four major areas-physical infrastructure, scheduling and staffing, transportation and food service, and health and behavioural policies."

2.11. COVID-19 Leading to the Introduction of Various Digital App in Education System

Among many of the Covid-19 lockdown, a digital divide in the Indian conventional Education system.All the education institutes and universities have been closed for almost three months now. Therefore, these institutes turn their hands towards the Ed-Tech industry when coronavirus forced institutions to shut down. This industry in India has had an adoption problem for a very long time. Despite good initial tactics to impress colleges, teachers and parents for E-classes are still dubious in accepting it on a massive scale. While private institutions have adopted this feature and started taking digital sessions, students in the government institutions are left behind. It took a pandemic for the government to understand that India's Education system needs a technology boost. As soon as India adopted the national lockdown, there is an increase in user registrations and traffic on the EdTech platforms. A study revealed by the top learning platforms that there is 26% increase in the user registrations between April and May compared to the year before.

Major steps are taken by the different state governments, for instance, the Chhattisgarh Government launched the *PadhaiTuharDwar* (Education to your doorstep) portal. This allows teachers and students to register online, where the online classes will take place in order not to stop the learning. But sudden digitalization for everyone cannot be an easy jump. There are many districts where there is a lack of digitalization and network access.

On the other hand, when private institutions are adapting this online platform quickly. India's EdTech market leader Byju's saw three times increase in the web traffic and number of students accessing its app. Other startup EdTech platforms are also growing exponentially at this time. Now, where the use of EdTech applications is on the hike, the exam preparation platforms **GradeUp** has launched campaigns such as *PadhaiNhiRukegi* and **Toppr,** which offers a platform where students prepare for entrance exams like IIT JEE, NEET, BITSAT saw the 100% growth in the monthly paid users. Everyone talks about the growth of India's online Education System without working on the present situation.

2.12.How can you succeed in the Future without working in the Present?

According to the **Indian government national sample survey,** less than *one-fourth* of the households have internet access. The **telecom regulatory authority of India** indicates that 78% of the Indians have mobile phones, out of which only 57% reside in the rural area where the bulk of the population resides. A recent survey by **Quantum Satis** shows that out of 7500 students, 72.6% use the mobile hotspot feature for internet connectivity and 97% of them face signal issues, only 15% use the broadband connection. Even before coming up to the situation of lack of gadget availability and an internet connection, there are more issues to consider about such as electricity. **Rural areas are the ones who face the power supply problem.** 16% received 1-8 hours of electricity daily, 33% received 9-12 hours and only 47% received more than 12 hours. Besides this, some schools also provide mid-day meals to the family below the poverty line. They act as a lifesaver for those people. But due to pandemic around 9.12 crore, Indian children lost access to midday meals. *It's tragic right!*The Delhi government reached out for some plan under "Learning with Human Scheme" to maintain the digital divide.

- The teacher will guide students through Whatsapp from KG to 8th Grade.
- The teacher will share the study material on Whatsapp for 9th-10th class students.
- The teacher will take online sessions for 11th-12th class students.

This pandemic brings the large diversion in India's Education system but the future of this sector depends on how the government will provide this system to the largely under-served population of this country. To be able to afford an education at a low cost is naturally a priority for every individual.

2.13. Effects of COVID-19 in Indian Education System

Among its many effects, the COVID-19 lockdown has also been a dampener on India's conventional education system. All educational institutions have been closed for almost three months now. While private schools are getting creative and teaching through conference calls, students in government schools are being left behind. It took a pandemic for the Indian government to realize that its approach to education needs a huge technology boost. Take for instance the government of the state of Chhattisgarh in India's center-east. It launched the *PadhaiTuharDwar* (Education at Your Doorstep) portal. School teachers and their students can register on the portal through their mobile numbers and some basic information. It allows teachers to conduct online classes and upload study material. But the sudden digitization has not been an easy leap for all. More than 2 million students have registered on the portal, according to official data. But that doesn't really reflect the truth on the ground. Over 180,000 teachers registered on the portal. But only 557 online classes have been conducted for students from Class 1 to 12. The teachers are now forced to run a digital classroom with no training whatsoever, not to mention the obstacles due to an unreliable power supply."The portal should be converted into a user-friendly co-interactive app," GayatriDevta, a primary school teacher from Jashpur, suggested. "Because at this stage, interaction with each other while learning is crucial. That notwithstanding, it doesn't help that the teachers are struggling to use the portal on their own."

2.14. How far India is able to fight COVID-19

According to the latest report by the Indian government's National Sample Survey Office, less than one-fourth of households have access to the internet, and the number is reduced to a little more than one-tenth when it comes to households with students. The pandemic was dubbed a great equalizer. But as always, those without the privilege of smartphones and high-speed (or any kind of) internet are suffering. To be able to afford education at a low cost is naturally a priority for everyone. Since the COVID -19 pandemic has disrupted the normal lifestyle of people across the globe, the virtual world has come to the rescue. Amongst many institutions schools have also shifted their base to virtual platforms to conduct classes online. Consequently, catering to the needs of all stages of education from pre-primary to university level, online education has emerged as an alternative to ordinary face to face classes. Accordingly, various stakeholders such as government and private organizations are trying their best to assist each other by sprucing up their existing online platforms, apps and providing training to teachers to use these apps and platforms to the optimum level. Moreover, efforts are being made by both government and non-government organisations and edtech companies to support the school system to make a smooth transition to the virtual world. Upskilling and motivating teachers, organising counselling sessions for stakeholders such as teachers, parents and students are some of the important measures taken by the administration in the recent past. Making a continuous effort to provide customised teaching-learning material suitable for online classes is another way of facilitating the schooling of children. The Central government has recently launched the PM e-VIDYA platform, with 12 new DTH channels, one for each class to reach out to all stratas of society. These efforts have proved beneficial to a sizable chunk of the school-going population.

Today, even after a month of announcements and extensions, it is difficult to predict when schools will restart. Schooling is supposed to look after the emotional, social and behavioural health of children, which is diametrically opposite to social distancing.

Presently, teachers are trying to engage with online teaching and learning. The technology may vary across schools and states but as educators, we have to look at the implications of these new learning processes for our learners.

From live TV broadcasting of academic subjects, video interactions, online theatre, to working with special needs learners, it is all about embracing learning "anywhere anytime". It is apparent that technological evaluation systems, touchscreen paper corrections, digital books and smart boards have become the new reality.

Going forward, in the new post-<u>pandemic</u> environment, what will be required is a huge shift in mindset-both social and emotional. A new approach is needed to teach in this altered online paradigm.

Unfortunately, as far as the education of the rural poor students is concerned, they inhabit the bottom of a digital abyss. Governments will have to think very seriously about allocating more money in the <u>budget</u> for technical education in schools.

However, wherever students have been involved with online learning, their responses have been very good-this has strengthened the resolve of teachers across the country, and has inspired them to work harder.

But the role of the teacher has not been fully understood during this crisis. Teachers are as important as health workers because they are looking after the mental, emotional and social health of children at home. Although it is too early to judge how the learning trajectory will be affected by online teaching, it is very clear that future transformations will ensure that classroom transactions are complemented with novel technological tools. The new challenge is, how to keep thousands of children out of school if their parents are allowed to return to their work spaces-even if in a staggered manner. And, whenever this happens, who assumes responsibility for a child's safety and learning at home?

Within this new school/learning paradigm, it will have to be seen how best to engage the children not only in education but in socialising with their peers, creating safe zones to play, and, how to also provide meals and support families which are working. In India, home-learning on a large scale will be a challenge, essentially because of non-availability of equipment and network-connectivity issues, and the fact that parents may not be in a position to facilitate home-learning.

We need to ensure that teachers come back to work so that hands-on training can happen-since many of them may not be technologically adept. For many teachers, their entire world has changed: From traditional teaching tools to juggling with gadgets and software, they are relying only on their personal understanding.

If school opens in July or even later, 3,000 children cannot simply come back. A post-pandemic school plan is essential and has to be prepared. With a staggered opening, the government and school leaders will have to think of novel methods by which children can be assimilated back into the school setting. And this has to be looked at bearing in mind the normal school calendar. Perhaps the new education policy needs to be revisited quickly and recalibrated.

Some practical things that can be done are: Cleaning and sanitising the classrooms and areas where children converge regularly; increasing the medical staff and counsellors in schools; planning a new school calendar where any event with large gatherings of students/parents is avoided, that is, sports days, annual days and parent teacher meetings. There can be cancellation of excursions and inter-school events within and outside the city; reworking of school timings and putting in place of student attendance on a rota basis. School walls could have colourful, pictorial depictions and slogans that sensitise students on basic cleanliness and hygiene such as washing hands, and social distancing- although too many displays of pandemic visuals should be avoided as it creates anxiety in the minds of children. We need to ensure the building of a strong parent-school partnership, if social distancing has to be understood and implemented; conduct periodic workshops by psychologists, medical practitioners and counsellors to help sensitise the students, enabling them to understand the situation.

When students return to school, they will be the least prepared for any form of traditional testing- all such testing measures should be put on hold at all levels and there should be more emphasis on instruction and emotional development. Particularly, the students in pre-primary and primary-in the age group of three to 10- will find it very difficult to get into a routine because they would have been out of school for over six months. At the primary level, when children return, they should be allowed to have their own learning options-creating personalised portfolios and project-based learning is important.

This will enable the children to find a sense of academic freedom, which they would have missed in the restricted confines of their homes. As far as senior students are concerned, we have already lost 2020 and this situation may stretch to 2021, as far as regular school learning is concerned. Hence, it is imperative that when dealing with senior students, we should help them understand the importance of resilience and mental strength in order to face climatic change, disease, natural and man-made disasters and even rapid technological changes.

The pandemic has truly reiterated the much clichéd skills of the 21st century: Decision making, problem solving, ability to innovate and, most importantly, adaptability.

These are extraordinary times, and we need extraordinary measures. The states and boards will have to, perhaps, look beyond traditional board examinations not only for the current year, but also for 2021. There is no doubt that returning to school after this pandemic will truly be a disruptive learning exercise at all levels.

The outbreak of corona virus disease 2019 (COVID-19) has been declared a Public Health Emergency of International Concern (PHEIC) and the virus has now spread to many countries and territories. We know that it is transmitted through direct contact with respiratory droplets of an infected person (generated through coughing and sneezing). Individuals can also be infected from touching surfaces contaminated with the virus and touching their face (e.g., eyes, nose, mouth). While COVID-19 continues to spread it is important that communities take action to prevent further transmission, reduce the impacts of the outbreak and support control measures. The protection of children and educational facilities is particularly important. Precautions are necessary to prevent the potential spread of COVID-19 in school settings; however, care must also be taken to avoid stigmatizing students and staff who may have been exposed to the virus. It is important to remember that COVID-19 does not differentiate between borders, ethnicities, disability status, age or gender. Education settings should continue to be welcoming, respectful, inclusive, and supportive environments to all. Measures taken by schools can prevent the entry and spread of COVID-19 by students and staff who may have been exposed to the virus, while minimizing disruption and protecting students and staff from discrimination (www.who.int).

Today, children and young people are global citizens, powerful agents of change and the next generation of caregivers, scientists, and doctors. Any crisis presents the opportunity to help them learn, cultivate compassion and increase resilience while building a safer and more caring community. Having information and facts about COVID-19 will help diminish students' fears and anxieties around the disease and support their ability to cope with any secondary impacts in their lives. This guidance provides key messages and considerations for engaging school administrators, teachers and staff, parents, caregivers and community members, as well as children themselves in promoting safe and healthy schools. The purpose of this document is to provide clear and actionable guidance for safe operations through the prevention, early detection and control of COVID-19 in schools and other educational facilities. The guidance, while specific to countries that have already confirmed the transmission of COVID-19, is still relevant in all other contexts. Education can encourage students to become advocates for disease prevention and control at home, in school, and in their community by talking to others about how to prevent the spread of viruses. Maintaining safe school operations or reopening schools after a closure requires many considerations but, if done well, can promote public health (www.researchgate.net).

India is a vast country and huge numbers of schools, colleges, universities and different institutions like IIT, IISc, ICMR, MCI etc present. Million of students are taking education from different formal and informal institutions. In the present situation we cannot go out from house due to COVID-19. Our MHRD minister said that education cannot be stopped. So we have to change in our teaching strategy with the help of ICT. This is the time to transform our traditional class room teaching into virtual class room teaching. Corona virus may be stay for long time so we cannot seat quite. So we should think that how teaching learning process proceed smoothly during pandemic and after pandemic. For the teaching learning process during pandemic we adopt some new techniques/strategies with the help of ICT.

2.15. Online Learning, Social Mediaand Higher Education

For digital learning to overtake traditional, there need to be comprehensive need-based solutions available for the learner. The deep infiltration of social media and mobile handsets into Education landscape has become instrumental in propagation of online and virtual learning environments. The pandemic has significantly disrupted the higher education sector as well, which is a critical determinant of a country's economic future. A mobile friendly, interactive learning forum opens up opportunities for lifelong learning too. Universities serve as centres for research and innovation, community resources, and are agents of social change should ensure accessibility and affordability, through web-apps and applications of digital initiatives in teaching learning for improving the quality of and demand for higher studies in India. Lack of awareness about educational opportunities, dearth of trained teachers, Lack of electricity, connectivity and power, delay in execution process, psychological resistance to change are some of the barriers,

2.16. Integratingtechnology to meet the needs of student and teachers in the Covid-19 scenario

In 1998, UNESCO World Education report stated that student and teachers must have sufficient access to improved digital technology and internet in their classrooms and schools. Teachers must have the knowledge and skills to use new digital tools to help students achieve high academic standard. However simply having access to educational technologies and ICT tools does not guarantee automatic transition or lead to innovation. A probable approach to introduce innovation rests with the development of an extensive digital ecosystem with emphasis on use of reliable pedagogical principles and strategies in the light of current needs of students. A multi-pronged strategy must be adopted by Educational institutions to manage the crisis, modernize their technological tools, change teacher's role and build a resilient Indian education system. Connectivity, E-learning, digital classrooms, massive open online courses MOOCs, massive open online laboratories, online certifications and distance learning programmes should be implemented to take learning beyond the four walls of a classroom. This process naturally necessitates gradual transitions from century old teaching practices and taking tentative steps toward implementing new ones driven by technology. There are challenges and we need to keep our students foremost in our minds

1. Learning community including teachers and students has witnessed extensive and considerable innovation in the field of education, involving on-line learning, blended learning, MOOCS, collaborative learning in the last few years. Nevertheless teachers in most schools in India have been engaged with conventional method of teaching.An experimental, critical, pragmatic approach to teaching should be adopted by teachers. They should create more effective learning environment, encourage students' participation, and help them improve their learning skills and habits. Teachers thus are to be adequately prepared to integrate audio visual aid and technology and use them as resources to plan, and organize the teaching learning process.Opportunities should be created to work and share knowledge in more open, dynamic, facilitating environment where students will be less passively dependent on teachers and assume more responsibility for their own teaching and learning.
2. Teaching Learning in this ever changing demand of the world should be determined in the light of teachers' knowledge not only about the students but the technological environment in which they will be

communicating with their students. Teachers should have the critical thinking ability, communication skills and aptitude for making use of the available resources to coherently and efficiently incorporate the new educational technology into their classrooms. An enriched and upgraded educational materials and learning environment should be made available to students. Educational Technology and Teacher Education have shared a disputed relationship in the conventional method of teaching. Most teachers both pre-service and in-service are not trained. The barriers hindering access to quality technology based education that facilitate their effective application in teaching and learning in schools and colleges should be overcome through digital literacy made possible through "technological inclusion" in educational institutions.

3. The structure of schooling and learning, including teaching and assessment procedures, has been immensely affected by the closure of educational institutions. Open-source digital learning solutions can be adopted so that teachers can conduct online teaching. Teacher prepared teaching learning resources, a combination of lectures with learning materials, tutorials and other learning activities can be made available to students. As Laurillard and Masterman 2009 pointed out to 'scaffold teachers' engagement with technology-enhanced learning' an online collaborative environment, 'should provide a framework for a 'community of innovation' in which teachers participate both as learners and researchers in the development of new pedagogies'

4. According to Kothari Commission (1964-66), one of the important social objectives of education is to equalize opportunity, enabling the backward or underprivileged class to use education as a means to improve their condition." As such, Right to Education and Equality of Educational Opportunities must be accorded a central place in promotion of human development. To bridge the ever widening gap between advantaged and disadvantaged Inclusive education through technology should be developed. Technology is enabling ubiquitous access to education even in the remotest parts of the country. With an unprecedented increase in mobile internet users in India, which is estimated to reach 85% households by 2024, it is expected that access and availability of technology based education can reach even the remotest parts of the country.Non Implementation of technology based Education works as a strong negative constraint on access to uninterrupted quality education. Immediate measures should be taken

to ensure continuity of learning in schools, colleges and universities both government and private. This disruption in delivery of education involves ensuring inclusive e-learning solutions to learning especially for the most vulnerable and marginalized. Online learning and mobile-based learning can increase the effectiveness of learning and teaching, opening opportunities for bridging the digital divide between rural and urban schools and colleges.

5. Covid-19 Pandemic has affected every aspect of human life. Human beings since the past few decades have indulged in ruthless exploitation of nature, polluting air, earth and water and heartlessly destroying the ecosystem in the process. Nations with advanced technology, have implemented strict measures to contain the coronavirus, but failed to control the transmission of pandemic. We need the compassion not only for the victims of the virus but for mother earth. One of the primary goals of education is to provide an appropriate atmosphere for teaching academic skills as well as instilling values that would be consistent with successful functioning in the society. Children should be made aware of the problems that are fundamentally human like cruelty, distrust, ignorance, jealousy hate. Children are catalysts for change and must learn, cultivate, and enrich the basic human values such as truth beauty and goodness.

6. The effective integration of Social media and ICT into the educational system is a complex, multifaceted process that involves not only technology but also factors like curriculum and pedagogy, curriculum design, teacher aptitudes, institutional readiness in terms of having proper infrastructure and long term financial stability. The process of change for dealing with disruption in education involves activities ranging from the development of infrastructures, to making arrangement for setting up of educational gateways and platforms with educational resources and training programmes made available for teachers and students. 'Indian education system is the most diverse and largest in the world with more than 15 lakh schools and 50,000 higher education institutions'. The major challenge before the nation is seamless integration of technology in education system. Thee-learning platforms, SWAYAM and DIKSHA platform, National Digital Library of India, E-Yantra reaching learners across all states in India can further be strengthened to ensure accessibility to students. Continuity of learning in government schools, colleges and universities should be ensured.

Classroom learning should be integrated with e-learning approaches with the objective to improve the existing delivery pattern and pedagogical methods. A well-rounded and effective educational practice with proper pedagogical methods is needed for unified integration of classroom learning with e-learning modes.

2.17. Implications of Technology on Education Industry:

Artificial Intelligence (AI) and Machine learning (ML) have had a major impact in almost every sector in recent years. Big data tools can have a big role in the development of a technology-driven era of higher education. AI and ML based models can guide students by estimating their success rate to complete a course with satisfactory grades. AI system can also help students with special needs to get more equitable education, helping screen students with learning disabilities diagnosing reading and academic difficulties of any student, in addition to carrying out routine tasks such as reading passages to visually impaired students.

The education sector is largely lagging when it comes to tech innovation, and events like Covid-19 place an even stronger spotlight on inefficiency and gaps across operations. Edtech and digitization at large could greatly supplement the learning process. Beyond seeing a more seamless transition to remote learning scenarios, tech could help provide personalized learning solutions as well as new and engaging avenues for students to participate in school. However, the sector faces significant barriers to increased adoption of tech. These include privacy concerns, lack of specific talent to operate infrastructure, and inability of many educational institutions to make investments in building out networks. Regardless, as we look to a post-Covid future, we will likely see increased acceptance of technology in learning, especially in hybrid formats that combine classroom learning with digital techniques like live broadcasts and virtual reality.

CHAPTER THREE

VIRTUAL CLASSROOM

A **virtual classroom** is an online learning environment that allows for live interaction between the tutor and the learners as they are participating in learning activities. In other words, the virtual classroom is a shared online space where the learners and the tutor work together simultaneously. Usually, these interactions take place through videoconferencing. The participants have tools to present learning content in different formats, as well as to implement collaborative and individual activities. In this type of interaction, the teacher has the particularly important role of the moderator who guides the learning process and supports group activities and discussions. The most common tools you can find in a virtual classroom are:

- Videoconferencing
- Online whiteboard for real-time collaboration
- Instant messaging tool
- Participation controls
- Breakout rooms

Synchronous virtual classrooms have the potential to provide significant added value to online learning by addressing the needs of the learners as they relate to social interaction and psychological safety. They can also create a new standard in the learning experience that goes above and beyond the physical space of the classroom and traditional teaching methods. The virtual classroom provides an abundance of opportunities, especially when combined with self-study platforms (learning management systems) or when used in addition to traditional classroom learning activities. Unlike asynchronous learning environments, the synchronous virtual classroom allows for instant feedback, direct teacher-student interaction, and engaging activities to increase motivation and active participation. Immediate communication favours relationship building within the group, as well as a sense of community (www.vedamo.com).

3.1.Software/Apps for Virtual classroom

A **virtual classroom** is an online learning environment in which students and teachers interact via the technical tools provided by the software. Virtual classroom software is used by educational institutions to host classes remotely while maintaining the functionality available in a traditional classroom environment.

A virtual classroom holds real-time lessons remotely while offering the same collaborative tools and level of interaction possible in a physical classroom. Educational institutions utilize virtual classroom software to provide access to students who may not be able to attend in-person courses. Through the virtual classroom environment, teachers can interact with students and students can engage with lesson materials, view presentations and videos, and take tests, all in real time.

Online course providers may either offer virtual classroom software or utilize it to provide their lessons. Virtual classrooms may come as an integrated part of a **learning management system (LMS)** or integrate with one. To qualify for inclusion in the Virtual Classroom category, a product must:

- Contain live video streaming capability
- Provide screen sharing
- Contain an online whiteboard feature
- Provide a comprehensive online classroom environment designed for use by educational institutions as well as individual teachers and tutors
- Stream live rich media interactive presentations (www.g2.com)

Few top software/apps for Virtual Classroom teaching

- Zoom
- Cisco Webex Meetings
- Google Meet
- Youtube
- Adobe Connect
- Schoology
- Blackboard

Training of the tutors/teachers for Virtual classroom teaching

It is very much important to train the teacher for virtual classroom teaching. During pandemic it is not possible to train the teachers in a training institute. It can be done one or two hours online workshop where train the teachers how to install, use and make the content online by using apps/software and deliver lecture audio-visual mode.

Adaption of Technology

People resist change without understanding the need and importance of it and when a situation arises all should adapt to change willingly and unwillingly. This was the situation which occurred to teaching fraternity too. Indian higher education institution has used various pedagogy for innovation, development and engagement of students. Many faculties have resisted the change when they had been asked to take virtual classes for students. And a couple of training was provided by the management of the institutions hence faculty will not face any difficulties on the same. As everything is your mindset, the faculty has to change their mindset towards the virtual classroom and adopt technology for the betterment of students.

Engagement of students

Student engagement is always a big challenge for the teachers even today, tomorrow, whether offline or online. It has been observed that at the time of online class attendance of the students tremendously high. Students are getting more interest in online classes and they are actively participated in the class. They are writing assignments, projects, practicum with help of teacher guidance and sending soft copy for correction also. They are also getting notes, e-content in form of PDF, e-Books etc. So it is becoming more easy now and future to engage the students in learning (www.researchgate.net).

Faculty Experience

Experiences of the faculty directly and indirectly influence faculty engagement and commitment. All the faculties mind sets are not ready to adapt the technology for the virtual classroom. But after attending/ watching different types of online workshops, YouTube videos they are ready to take the online classes. As they started experiencing it, it becomes like a habit, they started loving teaching students online.

The right platform

Choosing the right platform for virtual classroom is not an easy task. All the software / apps are not safe for online classes. Some of the institution using whatsapp for only audio and video recorded class. Some of the institutions are using Cisco Webex Meetings app for virtual classroom teaching. It is extremely helpful for the higher education.

Schools (some) are using video conferencing platforms like Zoom and Google Hangouts to conduct classes. Some others have moved classes to Microsoft Teams. Many teachers find these tools extremely helpful to make classes even more engaging than regular classroom while others are struggling (indianexpress.com).

Problems related online classes

- Internet facilities 4G/Wifi till now not available all the corners of the country.
- For the online classes every student doesn't have Electronic gadgets like smart phone, laptop and computers.
- All teachers are not train for taking online classes.
- Few teachers don't want to change their mindset for online classes.
- Students are more shifting towards online learning rather than textbook reading.
- Proper monitoring required from the parent side as well as teachers side stop the misuse of electronic gadgets by the students.
- Some time waste our valuable time to connect the link/login for the live session.
- For that students are feeling bore some time etc.

Management for online classes

COVID-19 pandemic is not only our country problem but it is world problem. In this situation, if we want to keep our learning continue so we have to transform our traditional learning and teaching strategy to virtual classroom teaching. Government of India has taken lots of initiative for that. Different institution of India like Universities, colleges, schools, NGO and private sectors continuously organising national/international webinars or workshops for train the teachers/scholars how we keep teaching-learning during and after pandemic scenario. By attending different webinars or workshops we can easily learn how to take online classes, how to make Google content and share with the students.

Advantages, disadvantages of online classrooms

The online classes, whatever the enabling technology, are only as good as the teachers and the ability of the students to grasp the new teaching technique. One of the teachers felt students are actually more responsive and active in online classrooms, compared to when they are in physical ones. "This could be because this is a new concept and they are excited to explore it with the teachers. They also don't get distracted by their classmates, which frequently happens in a regular class."

Teachers do find the absence of a blackboard a disadvantage and network connectivity a constant problem. "We miss the clarity that a blackboard gives us, we are kind of making do with the virtual whiteboard on Zoom." (indianexpress.com)

The use of ICT techniques in learning/teaching features a very positive influence on a student's learning capabilities also. It is established that students reflect during a very positive manner towards work and education once they are using computers to finish tasks given to them, encouraging and motivating them to soak in the knowledge. Students who used technology to find out in class have an increased self-esteem and self-confidence. Here are ways how children/students can benefit from this methodology in the times to come:

- The barrier this technology breaks is both linguistic and geographic as the information can be shared quickly and efficiently over the cloud thus, providing them access to quality education anytime and anywhere.
- The ICT methods are very effective in clearing the core concepts of the topic matter; this has been proven in enhancing the scholars level of understanding and retaining the knowledge.
- This method makes content more enjoyable thorough engaging narratives and top quality animation, making the entire session more interactive. This improves the retention capacity of the students, brings in more focus and makes the whole process enjoyable.
- The content is often tweaked to feature value to the training curve of the scholar counting on the shortcoming of a student.
- Active and independent learning are forte of this method which inculcates self-responsibility and maturity for learning
- The spatial reasoning capacity of a student gets sharpened over a period of your time and therefore the ability to unravel complex geometric questions without counting on formulas get a formidable boost.
- The child's progresses are often mapped within the sort of a electronic journal which can help teachers and students to spot the strong and weak points. ICT based learning not just assumes an important part during a student's scholastic development yet perceives the youngster's

subjective, social and enthusiastic advancement essentially. Through refined and present day systems, such as, video conferencing, computer game and 3D animation, it empowers students and teachers to figure together in ways in which mirror a comprehensively constructive way to deal with training. Also, it augments the student's quick learning environment, offering extraordinary chances to push learning past the bounds of the classroom.

Improves engagement

When technology is integrated into lessons, students are expected to be more curious about the themes they're studying. Technology provides different opportunities to form learning more fun and enjoyable in terms of teaching same things in new ways. For instance, delivering teaching through gamification, taking students on virtual field trips and using other online learning resources. What is more, technology can encourage a more active participation within the learning process which may be hard to realize through a standard lecture environment.

Improves knowledge retention

Students, who are engaged and curious about things they're studying, are expected to possess far better knowledge retention. As mentioned before, technology can help to encourage active participation within the classroom which is also a really important factor for increased knowledge retention. Different sorts of technology are often wont to experiment with and choose what works best for college kids in terms of retaining their knowledge.

Encourages individual learning

No one learns within the same way due to different learning styles and different abilities. Technology provides great opportunities for creating learning simpler for everybody with different needs. For example, students can learn at their own speed, review difficult concepts or skip ahead if they have to. What is more, technology can provide more opportunities for struggling or disabled students. Access to the web gives students access to a broad range of resources to conduct research in several ways, which successively can increase the engagement.

Encourages collaboration

Students can practice collaboration skills by getting involved in several online activities, for instance, performing on different projects by collaborating with others on forums or by sharing documents on their virtual learning environments. Technology can encourage collaboration with students within the same classroom; same school and even with other classrooms round the world.

Students can learn useful life skills through technology

By using technology within the classroom, both teachers and students can develop skills essential for the 21st century. Students can gain the talents they're going to got to achieve success within the future. Modern learning is about collaborating with others, solving complex problems, critical thinking, developing different sorts of communication and leadership skills, and improving motivation and productivity. What is more, technology can help develop many practical skills, including creating presentations, learning to differentiate reliable from unreliable sources on the web , maintaining proper online etiquette, and writing emails. These are vital skills which will be developed within the classroom.

Benefits for teachers

With countless online resources, technology can help improve teaching. Teachers can use different apps or trusted online resources to reinforce the normal ways of teaching and to stay students more engaged. Virtual lesson plans, grading software and online assessments can help teachers save tons time. This valuable time are often used for working with students who are struggling. What is more, having virtual learning environments in schools enhances collaboration and knowledge sharing between teachers.

Enhancing traditional learning outcomes

Educational policy regarding ICT hardware and software in schools has not primarily aimed to teach children the way to use technologies, valuable though such skills are (Hobbs, 2007). Rather, the ambition is that ICT use will improve educational outcomes across the curriculum, as revealed in exam grades and other standardized measures of assessment. Achieving this aim would indeed justify the considerable expenditure and transformation of infrastructure witnessed in classrooms in the past decade. It seems that an easy increase in ICT provision doesn't guarantee enhanced educational performance. Cox and Marshall (2007, p.63) observed that 'the contribution of ICT to students' learning was very dependent upon the sort of ICT resource and therefore the subject during which it was being used' - a faraway from generic or transferable effect and one that contradicts the straightforward assumption that because children like using technology, this in and of itself gives them the confidence and motivation that enhances learning.

Focusing on the few studies that rigorously contrasted learning via an online versus face-to-face condition, the meta-analysis did find a positive benefit for online over face-to-face instruction, though the effect was larger for blended learning (modes of instruction that combine online and face-to-face). However, generally the comparisons did not control for curriculum content, aspects of pedagogy or learning time, and 'studies during which analysts judged the curriculum and instruction to be identical or almost identical in online and face-to-face conditions had smaller effects than those studies where the two conditions varied' . Nor did including digital or interactive elements like videos or online quizzes increase the amount that students learned. On the opposite hand digital manipulations that trigger learning activity or learner reflection and self-monitoring of understanding are effective.

It can enhance interaction and increase student engagement.

Experts say that using technology in teaching and learning can increase children's engagement in school, quite an old fashioned textbook can as devices and apps are where today's students live their lives. This is a benefit for all learners as apps cater to all or any levels of ability and use various teaching methods to support learning. Apps also help to give teachers new ways of teaching the same thing, from games to virtual field trips. The National Math and Science Initiative found that the introduction of blended learning styles helps keep students focused for extended periods of your time and may increase engagement, especially for STEM (Science, Technology, Engineering, and Maths) subjects. In addition to the present, mobile learning has more room for personalization than most paper or physical resources and thus is often tailored to suit a specific child's needs.

Learning is not any more passive activity, it's active with applications. For example, like video games, level-based apps can foster a determination to urge to subsequent level. Combining education with entertainment can cause students to forget they're doing school work, boom, ninja learning.

Mobile apps help in systematic learning

Classroom apps are often arranged in such how that, it promotes not only a looking for learning because the child can track how far they've come and plan to advance through the levels.

In 2013 a study by PBS Learning Media found that 74% of teachers were in agreement that technology enables them to solidify learning in their lessons. The Huffington Post also found that "78% of Kindergarten through secondary school teachers agrees that technology has had a positive impact on their classroom." Mobile learning is accessible any time, any place. This means that teachers can address it to interact a learner at any point during the varsity day. Arguably more important than this, however, educational apps make it possible for youngsters to continue these activities once they get home, not just within the classroom. Indeed, anywhere can be a classroom. App learning are often done anywhere, therefore, it's not limited to in-school time. In fact, many educational app developers have many downloads; students are using them outside of faculty. Incorporating mobile apps in school can increase engagement and reduce misbehavior both in school and at home. Many apps even have embedded videos that specify topics more clearly than a textbook (the same textbook they're going to forget, lose or not be bothered to hold around). Also, using less paper is more environmentally responsible.

It is also possible that collaboration will increase as students can use these devices as research tools during projects and group work (I have seen this with my very own eyes in my classes, collaborating on apps is how today's students communicate, this literally puts learning in their own environment. Students can also use mobile applications to access a vast array of eBooks, PDF and other online materials.

Technology offers new learning techniques

Engagement can be increased by introducing varied learning methods and because of the ever-increasing amount of educational mobile apps; you can do just that with ease and without a huge cost as many apps are free for students to download. Research into learning theories suggests that games and puzzles, that many apps use, can stimulate brain activity. This may offer pupils who have 'hit a wall' within a particular area of learning an opportunity to tackle that challenge from a replacement direction.

3.2. Concept of E-learning in 21st century in Indian context:

E-learning is having the abbreviation of electronic learning. That means electronic instruments are used for learning. In wider sense the learning is facilitated by any electronic media or sources. E-learning calls for the service of the advance electronic information and communication media and means using various sources. In ICT, various media or sources are used for e-learning, such as computer, internet, microphone, pen drive, etc.

In India e-learning started very late in time but it keeps the position very fast. Indian education system still is in black-white environment. So MHRD tiers to develop ICT in school education system in every corner of the country. The positivity of that is the students will do the problems by themselves and the creativity will grow and also the classrooms become interesting. The teachers also can present the lesson effectively. For that NCTE include ICT in teachers' education curriculum.

E-learning is also known as online learning. e–learning encompasses learning at all levels both formal and non-formal that uses an information network–the Internet. The components include e-portfolios, cyber infrastructures, digital libraries and online learning object repositories. All the above components create a digital identity of the user and connect all the stakeholders in the education. It also facilitates inter disciplinary research and teacher training. During pandemic it is very much used.

Types of E-Learning:

Computer based learning: Computer-based learning is the term used for any kind of learning with the help of computers. Computer-based learning makes use of the interactive elements of the computer applications and software and the ability to present any type of media to the users and also learning without the need for an instructor to be physically present. Computer-based learning is also known as computer-aided instruction.

Internet based learning: Internet based learning is the term where internet and World Wide Web are used for any types of information. Various search engines are used for getting informations. Hyperlinks are most important element and PDFs are available for learning.

Web based learning: Web based learning is often called online learning or e-learning because it includes online course content. Discussion forums via email, videoconferencing, and live lectures are all possible through the web, thus enabling access to a vast amount of web based information.

Sometimes tools are also used for e-learning such as – e-mail, audio chat, online forum, web, video conference and online learning management system.

Positivity of using E-learning for teachers:

- it is very much flexible for using. Any time anywhere it can be used. Proper internet connection if one has then it is very easy to carry any electronic device rather carrying a large heavy book for PDF version or digital version of any lesson.
- E-learning based on learner centered. So, learner can get information about lessons and new information. They can learn sometimes without any instructor.

- Teachers can get easy teaching approaches and also different ideas for better lesson plan with proper learning methods.
- Sometimes one particular topic is not found in one book. Then a student have to buy many costly books otherwise borrow from the library. But from digital library one can get the topic very easily. Using smart phones one can save the particular document in the device storage for further use, free of cost.
- In online mode trainee teachers can get some lectures through videos. In distance education e-module will help get lesson from one's own place. Learner can grow self-learning habit.
- Teachers, during their teaching, can use different real life example with the help of online videos and how to explain the examples that also they can get idea form any online article.
- Digital library and kindle editions of different books are reducing the cost and save time in higher education, research & dissertation of teachers & scholars.

Negativity of using E-learning for teachers:

ax. Every corner in the country the internet connection is not so good. Though 21st century is technological era but India is a developing country. So if someone can't have the proper internet connection, mostly in the far flung areas, the teacher can't use the online lesson for students.

ax. Reading habit gives the chance to increase the level of imagination power and also help to increase self-understanding level. For a teacher it is very important to understand the lesson by self because the teacher has to give answer of sudden question in classroom situation. But from e-learning one can get easily any question-answer about any lesson. At this situation no one may try to think the answer by self. Using the e-learning system the reading habits are deprived by the new generation students.

ax. Due to privatization most of the private schools are facilitated the classrooms ICT and smart class system. Because of that student are getting very easily the e-learning environment from the beginning but in the rural area or some govt. schools can't provide the system due to lack of funds & infrastructure. ICT enable systems are very costly most of the time.

ax. To use the e-learning procedure, technological education and curriculum should be in the teacher training education. Most of the time the trainee teacher know the theory but there is no practice of practical work.

ax. Using e-learning students are getting habituated by self-learning. No face to face interaction is needed for the e-learning. But for a trainee teacher, instruction of instructor is very important in the time of practice teaching. That particular time online instruction should be avoided.

ax. Mostly students are doing their assignments from online sources. They, in harry, don't cross check the topic with any book material. Some time they don't get the topic from any book then they have to solve it from online help, but there is no surety that the information about the topic is correct or not.

ax. If teachers set up an example with an online video as a teaching learning material-(TLM) in a classroom then the use of self-creativity of the person is deprived.

Proper use of E-learning:

Now a day's e-learning is very popular. Though it is costly or is needs a proper technological environment, it has a wide implementation in every curriculum. NCTE includes a separates syllabus in school level with practical. Now the question is how to use e-learning in properly for gaining knowledge? There are three steps should be followed for using the e-learning process—

1. *Planning:* to use the e-learning what is one's particular topic that should be maintained. The main theme or keyword of the topic should be considered.

2. *Process:* not only from one site but also different sites should be followed.

3. *Checking:* if possible then the searched topic should be cross checked from books or any other sources.

These all are possible when a learner is well aware about the learning process and also truthful about gaining knowledge. Sometimes one tries to search a topic and (s)he got two different definitions from two different sites. The information can be fake or edited wrongly from the original one. That is very much dangerous for not only a new learner but also for a teacher. To avoid this type of situation one should cross check the topic as much as possible from different sources or from a teacher, but most of the time one is in rush to complete the particular work. Field work is very lengthy process but reliable for cross checking as well as gaining other experiences side by side.

From internet facilities or digital platforms any one can get new and updated information. It is very simple & interactive for a teacher to present lessons. For teachers', one should use the facilities for upgrading own teaching style, new style of learning designs and TLMs.

Presence of a teacher increases the confidence level of a student. Face to face interaction is very important for any student with a teacher. That why video conferencing is better for online learning mode, instead of a readymade video lessons.

3.3.Some kinds of E-learning Applications

E-Examination: In this application, students are administered many proof exams in the internet environment before the formal exams, which enables them to determine their approximate levels.

E-Drills: With the internet based drill software, it is aimed to create an effective and productive studying atmosphere for students. As students access these activities on the internet, they could study on the units through interactive multimedia software and reinforce their knowledge by examining numerous examples.

E-Book and E-Television: In order to enable the students to access the books and TV programs on the internet the contents of the course books and TV programs can be presented as E – book and E-television. Therefore a student of the system can easily access the books and TV programs as well.

E- Counseling Academic counseling: It could provide to the students in a similar format on the internet. Parallel to the research software students are allowed to ask questions to their academic counselors related to their course contents.

E– Sound Book: This enables especially the visually retarded students to listen to the course book contents and could be provided on the internet. Therefore, visually retarded students and students with reading difficulties could access their course books from their respective sources.

3.4. Applications that can help the teacher and students to communicate effectively for teaching learning process

Zoom is a video-calling app that is ideal for large groups because it supports up to 100 users for free. It is widely being used for meetings, online learning, and university lectures, among other things. The app has become immensely popular as people have been forced to stay indoors due to the lockdown. The free version of Zoom allows users to enjoy unlimited 1-on-1 meetings along with group calls featuring up to 100 participants for 40 minutes

- Zoom unifies cloud video conferencing, online meetings, group messaging and a software-defined conference room solution into one, easy-to-use platform
- **Security:** Although security has been a point of contention for Zoom, specifically during the COVID-19 pandemic, the company has committed to improving this factor. Zoom is making important changes to its security strategy and implementing new features. For instance, all meetings now require host permission and a password to join.

The key features of Zoom app are as follows:

- **Excellent support:** Zoom boasts fantastic user support to serve companies around the world. There's phone support available through multiple time zones. You can get a quick answer to your questions whenever you need it. However, the solution is so easy to use that you shouldn't have too much trouble
- **Scheduling:** You can also schedule meetings in advance from your Zoom app, which you can connect to a range of other calendars, including those from Google and Microsoft. This makes it easier to get everyone connected using the tools you love
- **Advanced features:** Another benefit of Zoom is that it's constantly updating and improving what you can do with the technology. Virtual backgrounds allow you to get rid of the messy meeting room in the background of your call. Additionally, there are even touch-up functionalities too for those who are worried about wrinkles
- **Immersive host controls:** The host controls in Zoom provide excellent control over how your meeting runs. You can create a co-host for your meetings if you're working with another consultant. Additionally, there's access to desktop sharing and hand-over controls too
- **Excellent engagement:** As well as delivering a futuristic and straightforward experience, Zoom also makes it easy to keep your team engaged with things like virtual hand-raising and other exciting functionalities.

Google Meet

Google Meet is a videoconferencing service to anybody who wants to use it, instead of just offering it to enterprise and education customers via G Suite. Google Meet is a video-conference-calling platform designed primarily for professional use, which links remote colleagues together for real-time interaction. On a basic Google Meet call, up to 25 people can speak and share video with each other at once. If you subscribe to higher Google Meet membership tiers, the number of people who can join a call goes up to 50 or 100. You need a paid G Suite account in order to set up and start Google Meet video conferences, but anyone with a standard Google account can join and participate in a Google Meet session.

How to use Google Meet

- To sign up for the free version of Google Meet, go to the Google Meet page. Enter your name, email, country and primary use for Google Meet (personal, business, education or government). Agree to Google's terms of service, and clickt Submit. Once you sign up, here's how to use the free version of Google Meet:
- Go to meet.google.com (or, open the app on I OS or Android)
- Click Start new meeting, or enter your meeting code.
- Choose the Google account you want to use.
- Click Join meeting. You'll have the ability to add others to your meeting, too

An **online class** is a course conducted over the Internet. They are generally conducted through a learning management system, in which students can view their course syllabus and academic progress, as well as communicate with fellow students and their course instructor. **Online classes** are generally self-paced, allowing for greater flexibility in completing coursework. Some examples of online courses are MOOCs, or Massive Open Online Courses, as produced by organizations. Many traditional universities offer online courses, including Purdue University.

Online learning is defined as learning experience in synchronous or asynchronous environments using different devices (e.g. mobile phones, laptops) with Internet access. Using these environments, students can learn and interact with instructors and other students from anywhere. The easiest part of this transition for Faculty of Education was providing online learning platforms and courses. However, we are meeting some persistent obstacles and challenges. Online course delivery, interaction, and data collection require stabile digital infrastructure and platforms, yet learning of some students across China and overseas is interrupted by poor Internet access. Students require capacity to conduct self-disciplined and self-directed active learning, and faculty require further professional development. Challenges also include lack of holistic quality assurance systems for online teaching and learning. The pandemic has revealed that quality does not refer only to achieving learning outcomes, but also to social and emotional development of students.

Faculty and Teachers are encouraged to choose appropriate learning platforms they are familiar with. In order to support faculty in their work, we developed five actions:

1. A line-up of main online education platforms were introduced to all faculty by email, we chat discussion groups, and school website.
2. Faculty were encouraged to share their previous experiences with platforms including Blackboard, TronClass, Zoom, Classin, Wechat group, and QQ group.
3. School of Educational Technology assembled a professional team for providing faculty-wide support. The team shared their knowledge and skills about different platforms and conducted online training. Further, professional companies were invited to train our faculty on using specific tools.
4. Learning online is a big challenge for our 2,096 students. The team informed students about changes, provided two teaching assistants for each online class, and ensured that every student is able to participate in digital learning. Special attention was given to students coming from poor regions and difficult family backgrounds.
5. The team collected information about all online courses, including their delivery platform, class size, schedule, and student readiness. Few classes were selected for trial lessons at a variety of platforms with the aim to pilot online learning strategies before their large-scale implementation.

Corona virus outbreak has significantly accelerated development of online education in Indian higher education. Internet, big data, Artificial Intelligence, 5G, and cloud-based platforms, among other technologies, have been put into service of education. However, a more flexible way of teaching and learning does not end up with infrastructure. Rather, infrastructure is only the first step towards a new paradigm of teaching and learning in post-pandemic time. This paradigm could represent a shift from traditional, teacher-cantered, and lecture-based activities towards more student-centered activities including group activities, discussions, hands-on learning activities, and limited use of traditional lectures. This requires conceptual and philosophical rethinking of nature of teaching and learning, roles, and connections among teachers, learners, and teaching materials, in post digital learning communities.

Full long-term integration of online teaching and learning into university curricula implies further attention to quality. Nearing the end of Covid-19 pandemic in China, we think that our further steps should be focused to the following activities:

1. We need to continue development of open educational platforms which allow access to the high quality of learning resources.
2. We need to conduct quantitative and qualitative research and evaluate current models of online teaching and learning, with a particular focus to their long-term sustainability.
3. We need to develop staff–teachers' capacity for online teaching, and professional staff capacity for supporting teachers and online systems.
4. We need to encourage cooperation between universities, international organizations, private sector, civil society, and other stakeholders, to promote high-quality online learning throughout the society.

Teachers are crucial for inclusive and equitable provision of high-quality distance education. They are expected to have knowledge, skills, and ethics to conduct online teaching, and that calls for more flexible and dynamic post-pandemic teacher education. Post-pandemic national teacher education could be composed of face-to-face teacher education, blended teacher education, and online teacher education. National online teacher education could be categorized into sections which provide learning opportunities to future teachers at all levels: early childhood education, primary education, secondary education, vocational education sectors, etc.

Online teacher education platforms could function as a traditional teacher education institute which provides pre-service and in-service programs. This could be supported by online platforms with rich digital materials and resources. Curriculum and pedagogy need to be updated, and should become models of successful online pedagogies that could be taken into future teachers' practices. Last but not the least, it is critical to build up an enabling institutional environment for sustainable national online teacher education. We need to develop evidence-based policies supported by guidelines for their implementation. To provide professional reference base for online teacher education, a framework of competencies for conducting online teaching, and other standards, should be developed.

In our post digital context, online and offline (teacher) education cannot be thought of without each other. Therefore, we advocate development of a holistic teacher education system, regardless of used mode of delivery, which could support present and future teachers in becoming more resilient to crisis similar to the Covid-19 pandemic.

Covid-19 pandemic has brought about a huge disruption to all spheres of human life. Chinese higher education and Beijing Normal University in particular, have responded to the crisis with reasonable success. However, we strongly believe that the impact of Covid-19 pandemic on Chinese education system should extend well beyond tacking the current crisis—it should also bring out potential development opportunities for the future. Our current situation requires innovation and renewed attention to more research, study, and reflection, about each sector of education in China and globally. It is only by doing this research within the pandemic that we can develop a more sustainable, inclusive, and equitable education after the pandemic is gone.

The online learning process initiated by the lock-down on a large scale is not just a platform for the students but a greater platform for the faculties as well offering many short-term certificate courses. There are many organizations and online platforms which have been offering various development courses to the faculties as well. The teaching faculties are making use of this lock down to upgrade their knowledge by enrolling themselves in various Faculty Development Programs offered by ATAL, NPTEL and MOOC. Many IITs are offering two week long online Faculty Development Courses which are a boon to the teachers the faculties have been upgrading themselves from the various on-line courses conducted by IITs and a good knowledge exchange process has been initiated which otherwise would have not been possible in the absence of the online platform.

With the available technology it is easily possible to convert a traditional classroom to an online classroom. Our education system needs to build that vision and break the stereotype thinking. Today almost every family in India owns a Smartphone capable enough to access internet and do video conferencing. We simply need to create that blueprint connecting students, teachers and faculty members via same. Classes, attendance can be easily managed using video conferencing. Instead of traditional text books e-books can be offered. Many reputed educational institution has already implemented this methodology and are providing education flawlessly even during this situation. A report by Google India and KPMG estimated that as much as 73% of the Indian internet users are going to interact in a regional language by 2021. There is a massive opportunity in the space of vernacular content. Amid this, having an English-only approach for the platform will limit the consumer base to a significant extent. Therefore, there is a lot of scope for business in the vernacular market, and further scope for them to play a role in bridging the country's digital divide.

A number of school ERPs like Entab, Francisian, Edumarshal, Fedena Iec have integrated with the free online tools like zoom, Google hangouts and Microsoft teams. For assessment purpose as well, a number of schools are integrating with free open source like Moodle or they are asking their ERP vendors to look for building learning management system. The Chinese government has contracted tech companies like Baidu, Tencent and telecom providers like China Mobile, China Telecom to create a National Online Cloud Classroom. The platforms run on 7000 servers and 90 terabytes of bandwidth, for simultaneous use by 50 million learners.

Grades 9 to Grade 12, students need immediate attention in terms of their syllabus completion. And if this lockdown continues even the lower grade classes will move more swiftly to online classes. The major challenge in conducting online classes is adoption both from teachers and students/parents point of view. On the other hand, I have seen some of the English learning classes for kids starting from 4 to 13 years have already started online classes.

3.5. An aggregate shock

As per a search conducted by Brainwiz, across India, the last two academic years have witnessed some unfortunate disruptions. For instance, since the abrogation of Article 370 in August 2019, schools across Jammu and Kashmir lost over 60 working days. Extreme weather and pollution levels forced a loss of 120 days across states like Delhi, Puducherry, Punjab and West Bengal. Furthermore, political rallies and bandh accounted for over 30 lost days. Yet, as one might notice, all these events, or 'shocks' were largely local in nature. A student in Karnataka was not too affected by the lockdown in Jammu and Kashmir. Even as students did not attend school in Delhi due to air pollution, students in Nagaland did not face any such issues. Furthermore, students across different states could have hardly made a difference to mitigate the hardships of other affected students. However, something is fundamentally different about the COVID-19 crisis.

The key difference between the current crisis and the other aforementioned crises is the former's aggregate nature. The crisis, for instance, has impacted (or has the potential to impact) Madhya Pradesh as much as Punjab. There are no safe havens. The last such 'aggregate' shock that comes to mind in the Indian context is demonetization. Yet, in that case, we knew that an active government was working behind the scenes to ameliorate concerns at the earliest possible. However, in the current scenario, the government is depending on social awareness as much as the society is banking on the government's preparedness. On the bright side, that also means that as a community, we broadly know what is to be done to ensure that one's neighbour does not contract the disease, or that a young student doesn't infect an older relative. As a citizenry though, are we mentally conditioned to face such challenges? Is the Indian education system promoting a value system that promotes compassion, empathy and discipline aimed at public welfare? To our mind, the sad answer to both these questions might well be negative. In such a case then, is there a case for an alternate approach to education to instil the intent to act selflessly in the interest of the society at large?

Sometime in the second week of March, state governments across the country began shutting down schools and colleges temporarily as a measure to contain the spread of the novel corona virus. It's close to a month and there is no certainty when they will reopen. This is a crucial time for the education sector—board examinations, nursery school admissions, entrance tests of various universities and competitive examinations, among others, are all held during this period. As the days pass by with no immediate solution to stop the outbreak of Covid-19, school and university closures will not only have a short-term impact on the continuity of learning for more than 285 million young learners in India but also engender far-reaching economic and societal consequences.

The structure of schooling and learning, including teaching and assessment methodologies, was the first to be affected by these closures. Only a handful of private schools could adopt online teaching methods.

Their low-income private and government school counterparts, on the other hand, have completely shut down for not having access to e-learning solutions. The students, in addition to the missed opportunities for learning, no longer have access to healthy meals during this time and are subject to economic and social stress.

The pandemic has significantly disrupted the higher education sector as well, which is a critical determinant of a country's economic future. A large number of Indian students—second only to China—enroll in universities abroad, especially in countries worst affected by the pandemic, the US, UK, Australia and China. Many such students have now been barred from leaving these countries. If the situation persists, in the long run, a decline in the demand for international higher education is expected.

The bigger concern, however, on everybody's mind is the effect of the disease on the employment rate. Recent graduates in India fear withdrawal of job offers from corporate because of the current situation. The Centre for Monitoring Indian Economy's estimates on unemployment shot up from 8.4% in mid-March to 23% in early April and the urban unemployment rate to 30.9%.

Needless to say, the pandemic has transformed the centuries-old, chalk–talk teaching model to one driven by technology. This disruption in the delivery of education is pushing policymakers to figure out how to drive engagement at scale while ensuring inclusive e-learning solutions and tackling the digital divide. A multi-pronged strategy is necessary to manage the crisis and build a resilient Indian education system in the long term.

3.6. The case for Education for Sustainable Development

In November 2019, the 40th UNESCO General Conference adopted the new global framework on Education for Sustainable Development (ESD for 2030) for the period of 2020-2030. The global framework for implementation of ESD is that the follow up to the worldwide Action Programme on ESD (GAP, 2015-2019). ESD for 2030 aims to create a more just and sustainable world through strengthening ESD and contributing to the achievement of the 17 Sustainable Development Goals. The framework will focus on integrating ESD and the 17 SDGs into policies, learning environments, capacity building of educators, empowerment and mobilization of youth, and local level action. Furthermore, UNESCO also plans to host a 'UNESCO World Conference on Education for Sustainable Development', after the world recover from this ongoing crisis. The Conference will raise awareness of these challenges, highlight the crucial role of Education for Sustainable Development (ESD) as a key enabler for the successful achievement of all SDGs, and create momentum for strengthening ESD in policy and practice.

ESD is aimed at internalizing the unintended effects of one's actions on others. By introducing subjects such as gender studies and environmental sustainability, education systems across the world are trying to ingrain among their students these concepts at a very young age. Through multidisciplinary, inter-disciplinary and multidimensional approaches, the overall objective of the exercise hinges around the idea of translating academic concepts into relatable real-life challenges and finding their solutions. ESD's focus on often ignored soft skills such as critical thinking, problem-solving, leadership and communication equip students with the right toolkit to deal with these challenges. These assertions are also backed by evidence. Evidence from across the world suggests that ESD curricula help students develop a deeper understanding of real-life challenges that the global community is facing. These include but are not limited to- climate change, socio-economic inequality, gender bias and peace-building. Through such a holistic approach, ESD seems to have not only developed virtues such as empathy and compassion, but is also correlated with better grades and a wider range of future academic and professional opportunities for students. It is, therefore, not surprising that UNESCO is pursuing this objective very rigorously and is working with policy-makers and educational institutions across the world to scale these efforts up. However, a lot still remains to be done.

As much as we might want to wish, the COVID-19 crisis won't be the last such aggregate shock. By not focusing on skills aimed at sustainable cohabitation, we have already produced several generations of adults who may not be psychologically equipped to deal with such challenges. Our best hope, in such a case, is to begin as soon as possible and churn out the next generation of community leaders who can think not only for themselves but also for those around them. COVID-19 might just be a trailer for several such challenges that await us.

3.7. Measures for Continuous Education

- Immediate measures are essential to ensure continuity of learning in government schools and universities. Open-source digital learning solutions and Learning Management Software should be adopted so teachers can conduct teaching online. The DIKSHA platform, with reach across all states in India, can be further strengthened to ensure accessibility of learning to the students.

- Inclusive learning solutions, especially for the most vulnerable and marginalized, need to be developed. With a rapid increase of mobile internet users in India, which is expected to reach 85% households by 2024, technology is enabling ubiquitous access and personalization of education even in the remotest parts of the country. This can change the schooling system and increase the effectiveness of learning and teaching, giving students and teachers multiple options to choose from. Many inspirational districts have initiated innovative, mobile-based learning models for effective delivery of education, which can be adopted by others.

- Strategies are required to prepare the higher education sector for the evolving demand–supply trends across the globe—particularly those related to the global mobility of students and faculty and improving the quality of and demand for higher studies in India. Further, immediate measures are required to mitigate the consequences of the pandemic on job offers, internship programs, and research projects.

- It is also important to reconsider the current delivery and pedagogical methods in school and higher education by seamlessly integrating classroom learning with e-learning modes to build a unified learning system. The major challenge in EDTech reforms at the national level is the seamless integration of technology in the present Indian education system, which is the most diverse and largest in the world with more than 15 lakhs schools and 50,000 higher education institutions. Further, it is also important to establish quality assurance mechanisms and quality benchmark for online learning developed and offered by India HEIs as well as e-learning platforms (growing rapidly). Many e-learning players offer multiple courses on the same subjects with different levels of certifications, methodology and assessment parameters. So, the standard of courses may differ across different e-learning platforms.

- Indian lore is documented across the world for its scientific innovations, values, and benefits to develop sustainable technologies and medicines. The courses on Indian traditional knowledge systems in the fields of yoga, Indian medicines, architecture, hydraulics, Ethno botany, metallurgy and agriculture should be integrated with a present-day mainstream university education to serve the larger cause of humanity.

In this time of crisis, a well-rounded and effective educational practice is what's needed for the capacity-building of young minds. It will develop skills that will drive their employability, productivity, health, and well-being in the decades to come, and ensure the overall progress of India. The Covid- 19 pandemic has sparked a global realization that our current way of life does not work. It has broken our perception of what is normal and deconstructed society as we know it. One such critical area, where the necessity for change has become evident, is education. The effects of the corona virus and thereby its preventive measures, has upended the life of students, parents and teachers.

The clear disruption in the 'normal' functioning of education has placed an emphasis on many questions, which were previously asked and subsequently left unanswered. So, what could the present effects of this global pandemic mean for the longer term of education?

3.8. Factors affecting the evolution of the education system

To answer these questions, which pertain to modernization and efficiency, a lot of factors must be considered. Given the period we've spent in lockdown and the observations of our abrupt transition to online learning, we've found the time to think and the direction in which we must apply our efforts. We've not only been given a chance to rethink the education sector, but also the opportunity to visualize how it can evolve in tandem with our changing world.

- **A change in the purpose of learning**

The course of learning and the way curriculum is taught may change. Aspects that were once considered fundamental to education may be revised to largely accommodate life skills of the future. Not just careers, but residents of the future as well will require skills like resilience, adaptability, collaboration, communication, empathy, creativity and emotional intelligence. Learning in schools will have a replacement purpose, and it'll be a serious deviation from the information-focused education of today.

- **The utilization of innovative methods of education**

Aside from the disruption faced thanks to the novel corona virus, education in our developing world has experienced some major changes. Yet, even within the face of rapid innovation, we've yet to shift the way during which we impart education. Learning is the acquisition of knowledge, but it doesn't have to solely occur through age-old methods that do not utilize the highest potential of the brain. Instead of being taught, can students be given an experience that influences their learning? Approaches like integrated learning and experiential learning, with greater implementation of technology, will power the future the education in schools.

- **A tighter relationship with technology**

In the face of a crippling pandemic, technology has emerged as a major lifesaver. Communication is a major key to our interconnected existence and technology is the driving force that maintains our connections. For education, meaning creating content and delivery systems that harness and utilize technology to its fullest. Perhaps, education may become more flexible and accessible, relinquishing its over-reliance on rigid structures that we currently consider necessary. Additionally, the present generations of faculty students are generation Z and alpha.

They are generations that are defined by their use of technology; it has become an extension of their consciousness and they do not know a world without it. The future of education will find no room to ignore the use of technology since it's going to alright be the simplest platform to empower learning in an age that is integrating technology as a way of life. These generations could influence the evolution of education, as they themselves are the ones majorly impacted by the pandemic and are in the best position to learn and grow from it.

- **A focus on bigger issues**

How will we ask students to go back to a way of life that compromises their physiological, emotional and mental health? Will we still ask students to get up to attend school at a time when their brains aren't suitably active? Will we teach students about protecting the environment while asking them to sit in buses that move through traffic and leave a large carbon footprint? The world could require a special focus tomorrow than it does today. Perhaps, education post-Covid- 19 will embrace learning from science and emphasize a greater specialize in issues that endanger our health, society, life and earth.

Covid-19 may have been the catalysis for a change that has been long pending. What we'll witness within the aftermath of this global health crisis may very likely be the adoption of approaches that were sought in it. Perhaps, the world may never go back to what it was pre-pandemic. But we can count on it to adapt to the future, irrespective of what it contains.

The severe crisis that Humanity today is witnessing all over the world due to the spread of coronavirus threatens the very existence and continuity of the human life on Earth.Schools and colleges across the nation have been closed down since the third week of March as a measure to contain the spread of coronavirus. Board examinations, school admissions for pre-primary and primary classes, entrance tests for various courses, admissions to colleges and universities and competitive examinations, economic and social activities, everything has come to an abrupt standstill. Closure of educational institutions is having a detrimental impact on the continuity of learning.For millions of learners regular teaching and learning has been intermittently disrupted. Many educational institutions due to Covid-19 lockdown have started online classes there by making teaching learning opportunities and resources available to learners. However only a few private schools in urban areas have been able to adopt online teaching approaches. Huge numbers of students in government schools in both rural and urban areas are facing disruption in education as they have completely closed down. This disruption in education has to be tackled with the objective to ensure uninterrupted delivery of education with e-learning solutions. The crisis has become a grave problem and a major source of concern for teachers, parents and society at large.Educational needs of the weaker and most vulnerable sections of the learning community should be safeguarded with an emphasis on managing the digital divide across the nation. There is a need to establish a vigorous system of education based on the principle of equity and equality suited to the needs of all the learners.

3.9. Technological Revolution in the Pandemic Scenario

Considering the larger contextual environmental problem, the pedagogical setting in which learning is to take place should be envisioned with the aim to design an effective dynamic system of education based on technology. As life and work has taken a setback due to present Pandemic Scenario the implementation of technology, ICT, online learning and E-learning, in current virtual learning environments has become a necessity. While ICT based education has been a desired vision for the past few decades, the circumstance under which it is being employed makes it sudden, impactful and innovative. There is a growing consensus among educators and scholars that this 'long-cherished and apparently utopian, dream' will now finally be achievable owing to the availability and pervasiveness of the internet, smart phones, and social media platforms and Government's UGC, MHRD's effort to integrate technology in education through various schemes such as SWAYAM and DIKSHA platform.

Technology based learning is an innovative approach for providing well-designed, facilitated, learner centered and interactive learning environment for students. Technology use and integration as envisioned by NEP 2019 is to be pursued as an 'important strategy for improving the overall quality of education'. Three main components hardware, software and data should be an integral part of technology based interventions. Several studies and research reports have highlighted the potential benefits and opportunities of ICT use for improving the quality of education and restructuring the classroom situation. There is an increasing need felt to incorporate ICT based education to deal with the challenges of current disruption in education.Disruption is an uncomfortable proposition; disruption in education due to COVID-19 Pandemic is even more discomforting due to the massive complexity and the unpredictability inherent in teaching learning process. Nevertheless Disruption and Innovation should come together to create a remarkable and impressive learning experience. As Clayton Christensen and his colleagues (Christensen, Horn, & Johnson, 2008) suggested "Disruption is a positive force".

A multifarious infrastructure involving online learning platform along with provision for appropriate learning materials suited for all group of learners must be generated. Several support systems for teachers such as widespread access to broadband technologies, Wi Fi, professional development support policies for teachers, development of innovative, rich online learning materials, Open Educational Resources and adaptation of procedures to make ICT use easier should be developed.The prospective benefit of educational technology tools to enhance online teaching and learning should be construed effectively so that it has a positive effect on student achievement. Some of the common problems related to connectivity, maintenance of equipment and its safe operation, adoption of pedagogical strategies to enhance teaching learning (tools to assist CWSN) and utilizing e-content should be addressed.

3.10. Teachers in the Pandemic Scenario

The teaching learning Scenario created by COVID-19 Pandemic is completely beyond the control and influence of teachers. Nevertheless Innovation or change in teaching learning cannot be implemented without teachers. The present Pandemic Scenario has awakened the need to develop appropriate strategies to undertake this new teaching responsibility while integrating ICT in the teaching and learning processes. Teachers can enhance their pedagogical skills and methodology with a better understanding of the available technologies for online classrooms which will help them monitor student's academic success.There has been a technological gap between the pedagogical activities of the teachers in the classroom and advancement of the society. Technology is gradually revolutionizing our society nevertheless the teaching learning activities in most schools have remained apathetic to this transformation.The quality and efficiency of education in classrooms processes in most schools and colleges in India have been based on traditional method of communication. Teachers prior to the epidemic have been accustomed to a different set of rules, timetable and teaching practice. With the change in scenario they had to hesitantly change their routines and conventional procedures, pedagogical methods. The present challenge that teachers are confronted with orient them to get acquainted with accessible online programmes and ICT skills. The present need presupposes teachers to be well versed in subject specific knowledge and be equipped with technological knowledge and skill to assist students to meet the demands of the emerging problem. A comprehensive and responsive educational system should be developed to enable teachers to act as catalyst in the process of change.

The role and perspective of teachers, their positive attitude, preparedness and awareness has acquired prominence in the present Pandemic Scenario. The teachers should not only proficiently use modern tools and make students adjust to online learning process but should have a positive perception about its contribution in teaching learning process. Teachers face the daily challenge of implementing educational strategies suitable for increasing student motivation and participation. Students' participation with innovative programme in a classroom situation is consistently high when they first interact with the programme. Gradually their engagement level subsides over a significant period of time as they become bored and distracted. A temporary increase in student interest and engagement due to the novelty of the technological experience is expected initially but there is a precipitous decrease in student interest, engagement, and performance. Moreover poorly selected and implemented techniques have a negative influence on students. Teachers should seek ways to sustain their interest level.

Some innovative, intermediary solutions addressing some of the challenges include a digital whiteboard to be used by both the teachers and students to write and share their views and observations, or present their ideas. Presentation tools can be used to share visually appealing content. The online teaching platforms provide options for students to ask a question or share an experience. Groups can be created for discussions, online quiz sessions can be organized, and several other innovative methods can be used to bridge the gap between online and in class experience. (The Times of India June 29 2020).

3.11. Effective Technology Integration

Education sector is experiencing one of the biggest changes amidst this pandemic. The advent of online learning environment with a careful blend of conventional and contemporary trends in pedagogy has undoubtedly become an important element in this somewhat incongruous and confusing scenario. However relying too much on technology or ICT will 'make students mere passive recipients of unrelated "facts" delivered as easily by a machine or a textbook'. Excessive use of educational software in online learning experiences will result in repetitive "drill practice" learning experiences. Technology is not a replacement for teachers it is a supplement to a good teacher. Educational technology tools in the current pandemic scenario should be incorporated into the framework of what is currently considered effective instructional procedure rather than simply replacing teachers with computers and online content. Online teaching,Learning from Home LFH redefining new parameters in teaching and learning, has become essential to ensure continuous learning to students.Maintaining discipline, maintaining a separate silent room and a good connectivity, a quiet work environment, having handsets and laptops or other devices has become a necessity. The advent of a highly globalized and technological environment amidst Covid-19 Pandemic demands that new digital tools be employed effectively in schools and colleges for online classroom participation, to remain connected with learning.

3.12. Changing roles of teachers during covid-19

According to the changing situation to the whole country, teachers also have to be transformed as the ambience demand. Teachers have started class through digital mode. The teachers, who are not expert in digital learning and not to use the ICT effectively, would be able to face this difficult situation. They have accepted it as a challenge and prepared themselves according to the situations and face the difficult circumstances. They have to be completely acquainted with requisite tools and they have done everything to become an internet savvy. They have taken up the fruitful conveniences of ICT and social media for sustaining their online teaching learning process. They have arranged online class at home through the effective use of zoom, telegram ,you tube channels, google meet and other education related app. UNSECO has provided many useful educational tools for assisting both student and teachers during pandemic situation. These are schoology, seesaw, google classroom, class dozo and moodle. Teachers would become a digital specialist going through the critical pandemic period. It is the best time for teachers to show how much they are creative and talented. It is very difficult task for teachers to draw attention of the learners through online class. They can loss their interest and motivation at any time as they attend the class from home. So teachers have to be creative enough to engage the students in digital classroom. Covid-19 lockdown offers a golden opportunity for teachers to grab some new experience. They have got the chance into the field of ESL and TEFL teaching. They apprehend the feasibility of exposing to international teaching. They have given a valuable occasion to balance between personal and professional life together as there is no rush to school in their lives. They can save a lot of time for preparing themselves to deliver the lesson. They have played more than one roles like good communicator, facilitator, positive thinker, good listener, love evoker and delegator etc.

CHAPTER FOUR

REVIEW OF RELATED LITERATURE

There are not many studies carried out on the pandemic affecting education but the researcher tried to cover most given on the internet. Firstly, the articles online and e-learning are gone through to make the foundation of digital platforms.

4.1. Reviews of related literature

Frederickson, Reed and Clifford (2005) evaluated Web-supported learning versus lecture-based teaching, and Cavus, Uzonboylu and Ibrahim (2007) assessed the success rate of students using a learning management system (LMS) with a collaborative tool in internet-based teaching of programming languages.

Lowry (2007) also highlighted the effects of online versus F2F professional development with a team-based learning community approach on teachers' application of a new instructional practice.

Mentzer, Cryan and Teclehaimanot (2007) also analyzed a comparison of F2F and Web-based classrooms. Zhang et al. (2006) evaluated the effect of interactive video on learning effectiveness. Zacharia (2007) compared and combined real and virtual experimentation to examine efforts to enhance students' conceptual understanding.

A few studies (Bixler 2008; Chang 2007; Cook et al. 2005; Crippen and Earl 2007; Nelson 2007; Saito and Miwa 2007; Shen, Lee and Tsai 2007; Wang et al. 2006) studies the impact of promoting aspects of learner reflection in a Web-based environment improved learning outcomes. These studies found that a tool or feature prompting students to reflect on their learning was effective in improving outcomes.

Then, the studies based on computer-based instruction- the inclusion of quizzes, simulations(Castaneda 2008; Hibelink 2007), and techniques for individualizing instruction(Grant and Courtoreille 2007; Nguyen 2007) was carried out to see effectiveness in online learning. The incorporation of simulations produced positive effects in two out of three studies (Castaneda 2008; Hibelink 2007).

Kumar & Kumar (2011) researched study the result show that no significant difference in the attitude towards e-learning based on variables and significant different in ICT familiarity.

Omar, Hassan & Atan (2012) revealed there is a positive and significant correlation among learner attitude and e-mentoring also attitude pertaining to learning autonomy environment is contributing to learners and attitude pertaining to ascertain success of e-mentoring program and learns attitude are critical factors to ensure students would stay involve with their mentor.

Hussain, Al-Qudah & Matari (2013) in his study found that no significant difference in the attitude towards e-learning based on variables and significant different in ICT familiarity and also showed were significant difference in the attitude of students of the colleges of education in Jordanian University towards mobile phone use attributed to the variable of the university and in favour of the Hashemite university.

Rhema & Miliszewska (2014) had studied on 348 students and result showed that the experience and perception of technology-supported learning gather student technology for learning,skill,satisfaction and interested to academics, administration.

Behera, Sao and Mahamad (2016) conducted a research entitled as "Attitude of B.Ed. student-teachers towards E-learning". In this study the result indicated that the B.Ed. college students showed highly favourable attitude towards E-learning and also gender, habitat were existing no significant difference.

Takkar & Joshi (2017) found that there is a highly positive attitude of diploma Engineering students towards E-learning. It is not affected in gender, locality or social category of students.

Komwar (2017) researched the result show that the college student has positive attitude towards e-learning and also gender and habitat did exist no significant difference.

Gupta & Sharma (2018) in his study the result indicated that no significant difference between the attitudes of senior secondary school towards e-learning of gender, residential backward, stream.

Xhaferi (2018) researched the result indicated that did not significantly their personal variables like gender, faculty and age but were showed significant between teaching factor and e-learning experience.

Jena discusses in his article " *Impact of Covid19 on higher education in India*" (2020) that how the higher education system of India faced challenges due to the pandemic and moving towards the online platform. How virtual education becomes a more preferable mode to continue the learning process. He discussed the initiatives taken by MHRD (now MOE) & UGC. He also discusses the post pandemic crisis in the education sector.

Mittal(2020) discussed in his article the challenges and opportunities for Higher Education in India and stated the drawbacks of online education for the disciplines like clinical medicine, sciences, Engineering and Technology, veterinary studies, and several other disciplines that involve practical training. He also discussed in his article that adopting complete online learning is also becoming a health hazard for students in terms of diseases like obesity, sleep disturbances, spinal problems, anxiety, and depression. And also discuss the initiatives taken by the Government, UGC, MOE, AIU (Association of Indian Universities). The author also gives some recommendations to overcome this crisis.

Richardson (2020) cited adequate digital equipment, insufficient broadband access, and poorly trained teachers amongst a broader set of issues that impacted children's right to an equitable, inclusive education. The goal of the study as a whole is to provide policy-makers, administrators, and educators with research-based guidance about how to best implement virtual online classes for students and teacher groundwork. But the researcher has a surprising finding of the literature search, nevertheless, there were a few published studies covering the various facets of digital platforms for learners. Because the search encompassed the research literature across disciplines, it yielded enough results with all learners to justify a qualitative analysis. Thus, analytic findings encompassing challenges and opportunities with implications for students' learning are reported here, but caution is required in generalizing to school learners because the results are derived for the most part from responses and observations in other settings (e.g., medical, engineering, business and higher education).

Bacow (2020) introduced that "we will begin transitioning to virtual instruction for graduate and undergraduate classes." While the general threat is the impact of COVID-19 on the Harvard community (and the world writ large), it is specifically the class experience that is taken out of the ordinary face-to-face realm and displaced into a "secure" format of eLearning.

Bacow's (2020) statement represents a clear securitizing move from the outset, and the acceptance of emergency eLearning by the Harvard community suggests that the securitization was ultimately successful.

Weeden & Cornwell (2020) said pandemic precautions called "social distancing" or "physical distancing" has attempted to reduce interpersonal contact and thereby minimize the Under Graduate student of community transmission that could develop quickly in dense social networks like the university campus.

Remya Lakshmanan (9th April,2020) said on his article "How is COVID-19 impacting online education" that, the nationwide COVID-19 lockdown has forced K-12 schools and universities to close and send their students home which, in turn, has impacted over 91% of the world's student population. The closure has placed unprecedented challenges on governments, institutions, teachers, parents and care givers around the world. The closures of the educational institution due to the outbreak of Covid-19 lead to an unprecedented impact on education. During the lockdown, teachers are instructed to teach through online learning platforms (Abidah, Fehabutar, Hidaayatullaah, Mutakinati, Simamora, 2020).

Raju (2020) argued that there is require to adopt innovative teaching for continuing education and to overcome mental pressure, stress and anxieties during the lockdown period. The outbreak of Covid-19 results in the digital revolution in the higher education system through online lectures, digital open books, teleconferencing, and online examination at virtual environments (Kumar, 2020).

Tari and Amonkar in their article "Impact of covid on higher education in India" (2021) discussed how the outbreak of Covid19 affected all the sectors including education. The teaching, learning and evaluation methodologies have been completely altered by this pandemic. And also discuss the effects on higher education in India. Switching into online mode of Education could be beneficial if the process of online education does not create any digital divide. To give more emphasis on online Education they stated that the online mode of learning can be the best mode of teaching if it can be accessed by all the sections of the society. They also included that the Institution should understand the experience and issues of the students to study in online mode due to pandemic and prepare according to the further design and the study pattern in such a way that all students get benefits.

4.2. Rationale of the study:

The study intends to critically understand the issues related to the impact of the Covid-19 pandemic on higher education and the sudden shift of education to the online mode of teaching and learning, opportunities and challenges of online mode of education .The study also aims to explore the issues of social justice in the context of the digital divide in India. It gives major policy implications for Higher education after Covid-19 pandemic.

Research Questions:

1. What are the impact of Covid19 on Higher Education in Siliguri?

2. What are the major challenges in higher education through online mode in Siliguri?

3. How the economical background affected the online mode of education of students in the field of Higher Education in Siliguri?

4. What are the initiatives taken by Government to keep continue the Higher Education system in Siliguri?

4.3. Objectives of the Study

1. To study the impact of Covid19 pandemic on Higher Education system in Siliguri.
2. To study the challenges of online mode of education in Siliguri due to the outbreak of Covid19 Pandemic.
3. To study the effect of online mode of education on the students of Higher Education with respect to their economical background.
4. To examine the initiatives taken by the Government of India to keep continue the higher education during pandemic.

4.4. Hypothesis of the study:

Ho_1. There will be no impact of Covid19 pandemic on Higher Education system in Siliguri.

Ho_2. There will be no challenges of online mode of education in Siliguri due to the outbreak of Covid19 Pandemic.

Ho_3. There will be no effect of online mode of education on the students of Higher Education with respect to their economical background.

Ho_4. There will be no initiatives taken by the Government of India to keep continue the higher education during pandemic.

4.5. Scope and delimitation of the study:

The scope of this study was to study the impact of Covid19 on the Higher Education system in Siliguri.The study was limited to four higher education institutions in Siliguri for study.

CHAPTER FIVE

METHODOLOGY

The methodology of the study comprises method of research, population, sample, tool and techniques, procedure of data collection and procedure of data analysis.

5.1. Method of the study:

The research work was exploratory in nature. This research was both quantitative and qualitative research method. The data for the research work were collected from primary as well as secondary data available from various sources analyzed. The secondary data collected from books, research articles, journals, print & electronic media. For the study purposive sampling method was used.

5.2. Population:

The population of the study was all the Higher Education Institutes of Siliguri area.

5.3. Sample:

Sampling Size was 100 respondents from 5 selected Institutions in Siliguri area. Five colleges in Siliguri area were included in study. These are Vidyasagar College of Education, Siliguri College, Suryasen Mahavidyalaya, Munshi Premchand college and Trinity college. Samples were collected by giving questionnaire to the respondents. Total 100 respondents (20 from each college) given their responses that were included in the sample for the present research study.

5.4. Tools and techniques of data collection:

Self constructed tool was used for primary data collection from students. It contains fifteen questions. Earlier the investigator made twenty five questions. After the expert verification questions were fifteen. Each item has a response option on Likert 5 points continuum viz strongly agree, agree, undecided, disagree and strongly disagree with respective weights of 5, 4, 3, 2 and 1 for statements. As regard its content validity test was shown to experts from the field of education for obtaining their verdict on validity. For establishing face validity scale was also shown to eminent psychologists and sociologist. Its language format instruction and size were found suitable for respondents. All specialists were unanimous in their opinion hence test has a fair degree of face validity. The responses to be scored 5 to 1 for strongly agree, agree, undecided, disagree and strongly disagree respectively all are positive items, the validity and reliability of the scale are related to content validity and test retest reliability of 0.93 respectively. There is no right or wrong answer for any item. It is self administrated scale. It could be given to a group of students at a time. They take 10-15 minutes to work on it. It is a true point scale .these are SA- strongly agree, A-agree, UD –undecided, D- disagree, and SD-strongly disagree. The students give responses to each of the 15 statements by in circling any one of the 5 alternatives. The reliability of the scale was measured by test, retest method. The reliability coefficient in test –retest was found to be 0.93 respectively. The values represent the reliability measures of consistency and stability to a greater extent.

Secondary data had collected from the different journals, MHRD, UGC and the official websites of University. Data had analyzed through the statistical techniques. The researcher adopted a flexible approach to collect vital information through webinars, workshops, one-on-one interaction, personal observations, and considers the view of administrators and educators. The data is analyzed and arranged systematically in the academic context in COVID pandemic to put forth the major challenges the teachers and students face in online teaching and learning.

5.5. Techniques of data analysis

To collect data from the selected sample, the questionnaire technique was adopted. The responses to the questions were recorded by the subjects on an answer sheet provided with the text booklet and scoring will be done according to the manual prescribed. The data were again presented through tables, figures and charts. The result was presented for interpretation of the finding.

5.6. Procedures: The procedure of the study was as follows

1. Selection of the area of the study
2. Selection of the sample
3. Selection of the tool
4. Administration of the tool

5. Scoring and the preparation of the data sheet
6. Preparation of statistical table as per objectives and hypothesis
7. Preliminary consideration for writing the report along with reviews
8. Finding the result and interpretation
9. Giving summary and conclusions
10. Making the physical getup of the report ready to be submitted.

RESULTS AND DISCUSSION

In the first and second chapters, a vivid description of the problem context has been outlined along with the problem focus by sighting instances from different reviews and related literatures. The third chapter is devoted to elaborate the design and procedure adopted for the study where as the fourth chapter is devoted to organization and collection of data according to the objectives and hypothesis formulated in the second chapter. In this chapter it is intended to present an analysis of the result that has been obtained through application of the method and procedure mentioned earlier. The result has been presented in table followed by the discussion. The findings have corroborated with earlier research for confirmation of result by sighting research studies predicting the same or different results by including these variables. The result has been organized under differential analysis and study of relationship on the variables and between the variables.

6.1.Objective 1. To study the impact of Covid19 pandemic on Higher Education system in Siliguri.

Coronavirus disease 2019 (COVID-19) is a diseases due to SARS-CoV-2. It was first identified in December 2019 in China's city Wuhan. The first case may be traced back to 17 November 2019. Coronavirus is a sickness brought about by another strain of Covid. 'CO' represents crown, 'VI' for infection, and 'D' for illness. Previously, this sickness was alluded to as '2019 novel Covid's or '2019-nCoV.' This disease spreads all over the world and created lockdown all over the world. Due to this pandemic situation, all fields get affected. Any one of them is education. It also make changes in teaching learning process. Due to this lockdown, all schools, colleges get closed and teaching learning process stopped. But ICT tools come to help teachers and students. Online classes get started and once again education system get booster. Nowadays there are different apps through teachers and students are reaching to each other and completing their work. Different apps used such as zoom, Google meet, Webex, Microsoft and many others. There are different platforms through which teacher are reaching to their students through online teaching. And students are also learning.

Among the most negative impacts of this pandemic Covid-19 on the education system worldwide, according to the UNESCO report, the vital one was that it had affected more than 90% of total world's student population i.e more than 120 crores of students and youths across the planet, by April 2020 among more than 4.5 million peoples worldwide. The same impact was also found in case of India, with more than 32 crores of students, particularly, primary and secondary students have been affected by the various restrictions and the nationwide lockdown for COVID-19 which was enforced since March 16, 2020, as per Government of India. As per the UNESCO report, the same figures for the world were about 14 crores of primary and 13 crores of secondary students who were worst affected due to this disaster. So after observing the corona virus pandemic situation, social distancing and usage of masks began as the first prevention steps to control this critical situation with the declaration of total lockdown all over the country and globe (en.unesco.org). As a result, the education sector, both national and international, became closed, comprising of schools, colleges and universities, both public and private, followed by the suspension of classes and indefinite postponement of all types of board examinations and all sorts of entrance tests of schools, colleges and universities, thus, destroying the schedules of every student due to the lockdown which could be observed as an exceptional history of education in the country.

But, the positive impact of lockdown for India was that it has, however, compelled many educational institutions, the educators, researchers, teachers, professors, academicians and even students mostly to choose the online modes of teaching-learning process for the purpose of work assignments, delivery of the online lecture classes or lectures through webinars to students and even for conduct of various board, college or university examination, virtually. Not only that, in doing so, COVID has thrown fresh challenges to many of the educational institutions of the country and even to the entire country to create many new challenges and opportunities to strengthen their infrastructure, so as to prevent the jeopardisation of the whole education system of the country (Jena, P.K. et al, 2020).

Impact of Covid-19 on Higher Education

The impact of pandemic COVID-19 is observed in every sector around the world. The education sectors of India as well as world are badly affected by this. However, impact of COVID-19 on education has few positive outcomes apart from the many negative aspects of the pandemic .

Positive impact of COVID-19 on Education

COVID-19 has accelerated adoption of digital technology to deliver education. Educational institutions moved toward blended mode of learning. In encouraged all teachers and students to become more technology savvy. The pandemic situation induced people to learn and use digital technology and resulted in increasing the digital literacy.

Quality teaching has become an important issue today and technology can play an important role in this by modifying the interaction between students and professors, and students with the world outside their own educational institution. Learning materials are shared among the students easily and the queries are resolved through e-mail, SMS phone calls and using different social media channels like WhatsApp or Facebook. Students are able to manage their time more efficiently in online education during Corona pandemic.

Teachers have also adopted new methods teaching like through PPTs, video, video conferencing which are considered as one of the best and fast learning medium of teaching. Students are able to analyze more effectively what they are being taught and definitely learn new computer skills as they are have to do lots of assignment through computer or laptops only. Even those who are preparing for competitive exam are being provided with an opportunity to avoid online crash courses or classes on 50% discount. Due to Covid-19, there is no option without online education. As lockdown don't allows to open schools, colleges, so online education is only one option through which education can be continued. Covid-19 has trembled the whole education system. It appears to the education sector as a curse. It clogged the academic activities for a certain period of time. But educational institutions in India have accepted it as a big challenge and shifted the problematic situation into a fruitful one to provide a seamless service to the students to the pandemic situation. Immediate steps of Indian government have transformed the whole education system from traditional to digital form. Though the whole country were passing through a critical situation but the covid-19 pandemic provides a positive opportunity to introduce a technology base education system going beyond the monotonous education system. The whole education system have been updating with digital technology. The best suited learning mode during covid-19 is none other than online learning mode.

1. **Use of apps:**Different apps nowadays are used for online education. These apps are helpful for students and teachers to reach. Such type of apps are also used for meetings, online teaching learning process.**Eg. Zoom, Google meet, Webexetc.**

2. **Platforms for onlineeducation:**There are different platforms available for online education. Through theses platforms, online classes can be taken, videos can be uploaded, recorded videos can be send. So these platforms are helpful to the students as well as teachers. Eg. Swayam, Webex, etc.

3. **Use of different e-content:**Due to online education there is no time limit as well as place restriction for learning. Anyone can learn from any place and at any time. So many type of education any one can take. And different e-contents are also prepared for students. These are helpful for them to enrich their knowledge.

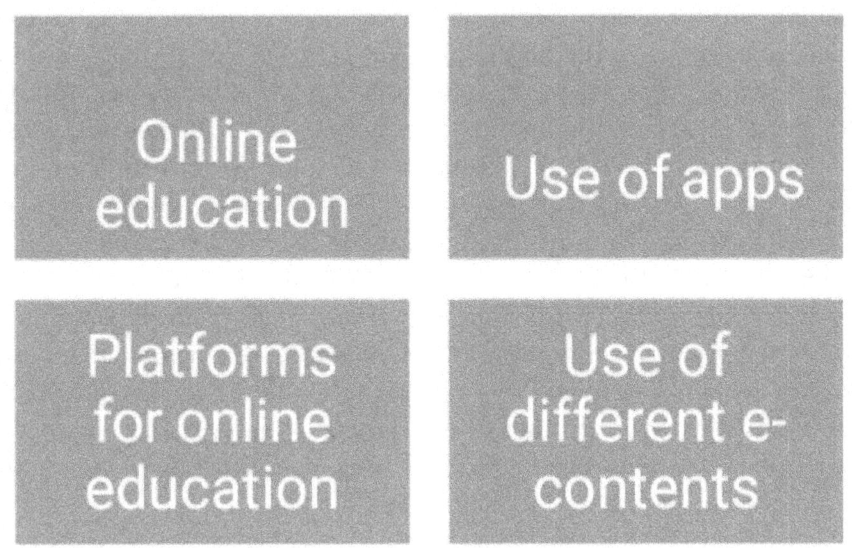

4. Enhanced teaching and learning: Technology helps to deepen the student's engagement in meaningful and intellectually authentic curriculum. By using technology such as digital cameras, projectors, computers, power point presentation, 3D visualisation tools students can develop critical thinking and problem solving. Students can explore more new things and also can learn and memorize concepts in an easier with the help of these tools. It also makes learning fun rather than a burden. It has helped in increasing creative learning in which the students can manipulate the existing information available to create one's own knowledge to produce a new thing. Online learning has encouraged more productive use of time which has helped individual remain positive inspite of being locked down in their homes. During pandemic technology has helped in conducting examinations for various courses and prevented wasting of precious year due to the lockdown. Various institutions has shifted to online mode of examination which enabled the students to appear in the examinations from remote area. Open book system has emerged as a new area which had remained unexplored for a very long time. This software can be used in future also when the institution may face delay in conducting examination. Classes in online websites/ conferences can be saved for later preferences.

5. Increased connectivity: Technology helps in globalization. Like in any other sector, in the educational sector also it is playing a very crucial role in connecting institutions in different parts of the state, country and even world to connect to institution situated in some different part. During the lockdown induced by COVID-19 pandemic when all the educational institutions were forced to close down, only technology helped to keep the students connected with the teachers, with education, with institutions through different platforms. There was a burst of activity with regards to online education. Government portals such as SWAYAM, e-Pathsala, e-pg pathshala, National digital library and various others has seen a multiple number of visitors than in normal times. When the seminars, conferences, workshops and meetings in physical form were curbed down, it transformed into online form that is webinar. Not online formal education institutions, coaching institutions for different competitive exams also started opting for online coaching classes. This has opened a new scope for students from poor socioeconomic backgrounds, backward areas and remote areas to get coaching from renowned institutions and compete with students who could take coaching by going to large cities in offline mode.

6. Provide accessibility to wide range of literary sources: Online platform provides accessibility to various types of journals which not only provided research journals but various other information, library from where any book can be studied or downloaded online. So students can easily access foreign journals, foreign books. It is a very cost effective technology which is quite affordable and accommodate a lot of learners at a time.

7. No geographical limitations: Online degree programme provided by IGNOU, Netaji Subhas Open University, Karnataka State Open University etc , Open Schooling provided by National Institute of Open Schooling and others helped students in achieving schooling and degrees who could not physically present in the classroom. During the pandemic many new institutions opened various online courses or programmes so that students don't have to waste their year.

8. Increases attendance: Attendance in online classes, webinarshas increased more than physical classes, webinars as individuals don't have to travel long distances for attending and waste a lot of time. Thus it saves a lot of time also.

9. Enhance students' engagement towards blended learning: covid-19 hasobstructed the educational authorities to take up the digital learning rapidly to provide the learning opportunities to the learners. They shifted the education towards online mode. It takes measures of new method of delivery and assessment of teaching learning process. There is a huge chance to transform the area of curriculum development, evaluation and pedagogy. As there in no physical and geographical boundary in online learning so teacher can connect a huge number of students in a single class at one time. Teachers are capable to make engage a major part of the students as there is no limitation of classroom boundary.

10. Affordability: online learning is easily affordable to the learners in comparison with traditional learning. It reduces the expenditure which a student does for a regular purpose like transport, meal, study material etc. In the lockdown period, students are not to come out from home to collect the hard copies of study material. In this situation, the one and only means was soft copy of study material. So, online mode of learning becomes the best provider to give out the soft copies of study material.

11. Improvement of collaborative learning: online is the vital means to develop collaborative teaching learning process. It appears a great opportunity to learners for expressing their inner potentialities, creativity and talent. Teachers also have got the chance to exhibit their teaching learning experience with diverse method and strategy. Teachers would use the collaborative teaching learning method among the faculty, teachers, and students through the effective use of online platforms like teleconferencing, virtual meeting, webinar and e-conferencing.

12. Provide diverse learning strategy: online learning is a golden opportunity to a teacher to successfully administer to diverse students with individual needs. Teachers have got the chance to personally fulfil learning requirements by the productive usage of ICT including assistive device and TLM.

13. Conserve time and place: both teacher and students have not rushed to attend the class according to daily routine. Online learning mode provide a lot of time for academic activities staying at home. Both they devoted more time to complete their educational deeds to prepare and develop themselves.

14. Competency indicator: online learning makes teacher more competent than offline. Teachers can use more than one learning tools to make their teaching strategy interesting and attractive. Because, online learning delivers a number of tool and resource which reach to the students as interesting and boringlesness. Online learning does not make the students monotonous.

15. Mark up digital literacy: people are provided a great opportunity to learn, use and handle the digital technologies. As a consequence the digital technology is increased among them.

Negative impact of COVID-19 on Higher Education

Education sector has suffered a lot due to the outbreak of COVID-19. It has created many negative impacts on education. Classes have been suspended and exams at different levels postponed. Admission process got delayed. Most of the recruitment got postponed due to COVID-19. Placement for students may also be affected with companies delaying the on board of students. Unemployment rate is expected to be increased due to this pandemic.

Other problems is also that not all teachers/ students are good at it or at least not all of them were ready for this sudden transition from face to face learning to online learning. Moreover, online learning has also been a problem to poor or lower middle class student who do not have any internet facilities. As many students have limited or no internet access and many students may not be able to buy computer, laptops or supporting mobile phones in their homes, online learning may create a digital divide among students the lockdown has hit the poor students who want to acquire higher education for their life very hard in India as most of them are unable to explore online learning according to various reports. Thus, the online teaching- learning method during pandemic COVID-19 may enhance the gap between rich/ poor and urban/rural. Some where, students are missing their schools colleges' life where they used to enjoy a lot with their friends along with their studies and their education and they also miss their extra-curricular activities.

1. Passive learning by students

The sudden shift to online learning without any planning -- especially in countries like India where the backbone for online learning was not ready and the curriculum was not designed for such a format -- has created the risk of most of our students becoming passive learners and they seem to be losing interest due to low levels of attention span.

2. Unprepared teachers for online education

Online learning is a special kind of methodology and not all teachers are good at it or at least not all of them were ready for this sudden transition from face to face learning to online learning. Thus, most of the teachers are just conducting lectures on video platforms such as Zoom which may not be real online learning in the absence of a dedicated online platform specifically designed for the purpose.

3. Rise in Blended Learning

Universities and colleges will shift to a model of blended learning where both face to face deliveries along with an online model will become a norm. This will require all teachers to become more familiar with technology and go through some training to bring them to the level that would be required.

4. In many instances, the amount of information, 'how to' guides, help and resources provided online can have a tendency to become overwhelming and confusing if not properly managed. It can be difficult for students and teachers to select which are relevant or important.

5. Students' perception about online learning

There are a few number of effective digital technologies obtainable for online teaching learning method during critical condition of covid-19.Most of them have made of a lot of stubborn to use .The modern technologies are associated with a lot of problems .These problems are the downloading errors, problems of installation, login issues, problems of with audio and video. Students are not able to set their concentration for a long period of time as it is a one way process .But a student is habituated with the two way process of learning where they actively take part in the learning .There are not enough amenities to practice and learn effectively. Students who are the habitants of village, semi town, small cities, and remote areas, could not use and handle the online learning classes. They are the appropriate students of traditional offline class. Learners face enormous problems for not handling the digital technologies. Besides, in these areas, thee are is not enough internet connectivity. So in this case, the time does not match with the teachers and other students and that's why missed the valuable class. Students, who come from the poor economic background, cannot afford an expensive smart phone, laptop, tablets, or i –phone .As to maintain the internet connectivity is highly expensive so most of them cannot buy it frequently. It is very difficult and challenging time for them to survive their daily living. In the pandemic situation, a large part of the people in our country have lost their jobs and become unemployed. They have been suffering from the daily essential commodities. Many families have been starving during lockdown period. All the family members are resisted to remain at home for the safety of their lives. The family which have more than one member but do not have sufficient room for remaining comfortably then how they get enough space to attend the online class. And the family which has more than one student, it is difficult for a low earning family to buy smart phone for individual student.

1. **Technological issues:** in spite of the several advantages of online learning, there are some negative issues of online learning like others. One of the most difficult problems is the internet connectivity. Both teachers and students residing at smaller cities and remote areas have been suffering low internet connectivity very badly. They cannot connect each other at the allotted time of class scheduled. They do not enjoy the online learning absolutely.

2. **Deficiency of teachers' skill:** in online learning a teacher must have minimum sense of handling the digital forms of learning. Not all the teachers, but a large number of them is not habituated to the effect usage of online learning tools and technologies. So, they need training for updating themselves with the latest technologies. Consequently they would be able to conduct their online learning easily.

3. **Insipidity to set on screen:** to spent so many time staring at screen makes harmful effect on health both teacher and student. It would damage the eyesight including other physical problems.

4. **Desolate attitude:** students have to attained class alone staying at home in online learning. This is a psychological problem of feeling lonely because they are not in traditional class room with a crowd of learners. So naturally they lost interest attention to the class.

The COVID-19 pandemic has disrupted the lives of students in different ways, depending not only on their level and course of study but also on the point they have reached in their programmes. The various suggested ways along with the drawbacks can assist the learning process to achieve the goal of learning in this pandemic situation.

As discussed above, major entrance examinations are postponed including engineering, medical, law, agriculture, fashion and designing courses, etc. This situation can be a ringing alarming bell mainly in private sector universities. Maybe some faculties and employees may face salary cuts, bonuses and increments can also be postponed.

- The lockdown has generated uncertainty over the exam cycle. May be universities may face impact in terms of a slowdown in student internships and placements, lower fee collection that can create hurdles in managing the working capital.
- Another major concern is that it can affect the paying capacity of several people in the private sector, which is catering to a sizeable section of the students in the country.
- Student counselling operations are also affected.
- Several institutions may pause faculty hiring plans for existing vacancies which in turn affect quality and excellence.
- Structure of schooling and learning includes teaching and assessment methodologies and due to closure, it will be affected.
- Technology may play an important role in the lockdown period like study from home and work from home. In India, some private schools could adopt online teaching methods. Low-income private and government school may not be able to adopt online teaching methods. And as a result, there will be completely shut down due to no access to e-learning solutions. In addition to the opportunities for learning, students will also miss their meals and may result in economic and social stress.
- Higher education sectors are also disrupted which again pave an impact on the country's economic future. Various students from India took admissions in abroad like the US, UK, Australia, China etc. And these

countries are badly affected due to COVID-19. Maybe there is a possibility that students will not take admissions there in future and if the situation persists, in the long run then there will be a decline in the demand for international higher education also. Isn't it!

• Another major concern is employment. Students those have completed their graduation may have fear in their minds of withdrawal of job offers from the corporate sector due to the current situation. The Centre for Monitoring Indian Economy's estimates unemployment shortage from 8.4% in mid-March to 23% in early April. In the urban unemployment rate is 30.9%.

6.2.Objective 2. To study the challenges of online mode of education in Siliguri due to the outbreak of Covid19 Pandemic.

Basically this is the time young students write entrance exams, consider which colleges to apply to in India, or make plans for studies abroad. But there's nothing usual about the times today. The Covid-19 pandemic has shocked the world. The pressure on students and higher education institutions is high. Schools and universities have been closed and exams postponed. Classrooms are going virtual and admissions for the upcoming academic year are fraught with confusion. According to UNESCO, over 320 million students in Indian schools and colleges are currently impacted. The pandemic has pushed the world to drastically reinvent ways of coping with the 'new normal'. After the initial phase of complete overhaul, it is critical to understand the short and long-term impact and future measures. Can India emerge from this crisis with a refreshed perspective and boost to higher education?

In India, the major challenge in rural areas is still a reliable and continuous supply of electricity. A second hindrance is network reach and connectivity. When focusing on higher education, though, a small percentage of people in rural areas opt for this, and those who are interested typically move to urban areas. According to data (as on January 2020) there are 650 million mobile phones users in India, 500 million of which are smart phone and internet users . In 2020 it was reported that the average broadband download speed in India is 41.48 Mbps. This bandwidth may be sufficient for online streaming of lectures, but data shows that connectivity issues cannot be ignored even in urban areas. There are many households that have access to smart phones but not to broadband connections. Though online learning has many upsides, especially during a pandemic, there are a number of challenges to consider. Studying online also makes students more prone to distractions like surfing the web or multitasking. In this case, students might not receive the full benefits they would see from in-person learning.

Another challenge to consider is the mental and physical health effects that students experience when using digital devices for education all day long. In June 2020, a Gallup poll found that roughly 30% of students were struggling emotionally or mentally due to pandemic response measures including the move to remote learning. Tactile and interpersonal skills may also suffer, especially in younger children where playing, socializing, and interacting with others is critical to development.

It's worth to mention that the current pandemic had never impacted academia so badly and causing shutting doors of institutions for all of us. The unprecedented and unheard situations don't require just the best teaching methods, approaches, and practices but need concrete and tangible action in response to all that we have. The natural calamities and virus-effects challenging times can never be isolated and we learn to survive with these problems in the future. It's true that we have managed and conduct virtual classes using ICT on various virtual platforms to cater needs of the students to impart learning. But, there is still a large marginalized section of communities and students who are hit the moist and tend to exacerbate the inequalities already existing in society.

Now a days, there is a new debate comes in fronts us i.e. Govt. vs. private institutions. Parents have more faith in private institutions, though the fee structure is high, because the private institutions have the facilities of computer literacy and other extra-curricular activities. In India most of the Govt. institutions don't have the proper infrastructure to avail the computer programs. Lack of fund and corruption may cause of this lack. In the other hand poverty is another important cause of the imbalance of the society. During this pandemic all institutions are arranging online classes for the students. Using different platform of internet, teachers are taking the classes. Managements take the initiatives for the continuation the education system. Most of the states in India examination is interrupted. To set up examination through online is very problematic. It is creating very pathetic situation and challenging moment for the students. These types of disaster take the education system one year back from its usual time frame. Not all students have the facility of online classes in India. There are lots of reasons behind it. Some of them are:

I. All the region of India is not internet friendly. Lack of electricity & internet facility in the far flung areas is the cause of absence of digital platform. Not only students but also teachers cannot avail the facility.

II. Practical and field work is not possible through online.

III. Because of poverty most of the parents cannot provide smart phones to their children.

IV. Most of the Govt. institutions are not running the online classes. In post pandemic time there will create a huge educational gap between these two groups of students- online users & non-users.

V. There is another problem during the pandemic is the over use of internet by students'. In post pandemic time it may cause of loneliness, lack of interest in playing, lace of interest of practical experience and increment of cyber crime.

VI. During lockdown children cannot play in free environment with their friends. It may cause of gloominess. Teachers also cannot teach the students in practical way in open area.

Challenges of Online Education

The crisis of COVID-19 poses a severe challenge for ensuring face to face quality education all over the world. But it helps to widely experiment with online education globally. The experimentation process started in March last week, and it's continuing till now. In this long time experimentation, there are many educators and research scholars tried to understand how online mode education was continuing, how much effective this experiment for providing quality education to all, what kind of problem faced by the students, teachers, and other members of the institution by an online mode. So, to understand this question and find the answer the research scholar and educators conducting much research program and written many articles. The investigators, reviewing these articles and revealed that the online mode learning program was continuing through suffering many challenges. Investigator also found that students and teachers also faced different types of challenges through online learning. After reviewing many challenges, the reviewer divided them into four-part, technological challenges, pedagogical challenges, and behavioural challenges

1. Technological challenges

Technical problems: One studying shows that technology-related challenges are associated with downloading errors, issues with the installation of different types of applications, login problems, problems with audio and video, etc. These types of problems create a barrier to accessing online classes, online studying materials. Etc.

Unstable network connection: The major component of online learning is internet connection (Adedoyin, O.B., & Soykan, E. 2020). Because most of the work has been done through online platforms, and online social media. Without internet connection, we could not access online learning. But in India, the major problem is the unstable internet connection basically in rural areas. According to the World Bank report (January 2021), a majority (65.53%) of the population lived in villages in India. So through online learning urban people are taking advantage to get education easily but one-third of people deprived of education. There are many studies that revealed that one of the important challenges of accessing online learning for all is unstable network connection. (Mishra, L. et al. 2020, Adedoyin, O.B., & Soykan, E. 2020, Kamal, A.A. et al., 2020). One study revealed that 79% of participants say that unstable network connection lost their interest during long-time online learning (Shetty, S. et. All., 2020). Recently conducted a study explore that half of the teachers faced slow internet connection related problems (OXFAM study 2020). Another study says that a heavy internet bill poses a big challenge for continuing online classes, basically low economic status students (Putri et al., 2020).

Lack of secure internet facilities in private, and public educational institutions: The use of the internet creates a big disparity among different countries. World Development Indicators statistics show that only 34.5% of people were used the internet in 2017 in India. It creates a digital gap between the use of the internet and access to secure internet. In this regard, providing online education to all in the COVID-19 pandemic situation possess a big challenge. A study conducted by NCERT (2020) reflects that approximately 27% of the students do not use the internet because they do not have any smartphone or laptop. On the other side, NSSO Social Consumption on Education Survey (2017-18) shows that only 4% of primary schools, 16% of upper primary, 30% of secondary, and 56% of higher secondary schools were used the internet. So, in this lockdown situation its make a challenging situation for providing online education to all. It also raises a disparity situation among the social group, and different socioeconomic status people. (Padhi, B. et al. 2020), which leads to inequality in education all over India.

Lack of technological device and infrastructure facilities: Technological devices and infrastructure facilities-related challenges are associated with a lack of the Internet connectivity and electronic devices. These electronic devices are laptop, smartphone, modem, smart board, computer, a different type of software and application, etc. there are many studies revealed that the majority of the schools have not any infrastructural facilities for conducting online classes. So, the majority of the online classes are continuing through the WhatsApp application (Dewi, 2020), (Gunawan et al., 2020), (Purwanto et al., 2020). A study conducted by NCERT (2020) reflects that 27% of students have not any smartphone. Another study shows that students are continuing their online class through their parent's smartphone, which creates a barrier to attend the online class every time, basically in rural areas (Athar, U. & Sharma, G. 2020). So lack of technological devices and proper infrastructural facilities are highly affected to continuing online classes in the pandemic situation (Putri et al., 2020).

Lack of technical experts: There are many studies revealed that lack of technical knowledge of students, teachers, and another member of the institutional staff also hindered successfully implementing online education in the COVID-19 pandemic situation (Putri et al. 2020), (Khali, R et. al, 2020), Alam, M. A. (2020).

2. Pedagogical challenges

The virtual classroom lacks major activities on the topics prepared and taught based on major constructivist, collaborative, integrative, reflective, and inquiry-based learning. The students feel bore and show no interest to attend the virtual classes. The class seems to be teacher-centered without any productive work and learning collectively. The teacher acts not as a mentor who helps students achieve the learning goal in F2F classroom teaching. It lacks real-world illustrations given in the classroom. The virtual or online synchronous teaching misses the fundamental aspects of pedagogy; curriculum/ content of what is being taught, methodology, and techniques for socializing children in the repertoire of cognitive and affective skills required to attain 21st-century life skills. One study revealed that lack of meaningful interaction with teachers, and a low range of innovative teaching leads a low level of understanding of the concept. It also found that teachers were unable to understand the learner's mood and change the teaching instruction to teach learners with their moods or interest (Mishra, L. et al. 2020). This study also indicates teachers were accepting that they are unable to clarifying their doubts and fulfilling their learner's satisfaction level by online mode. Other studies revealed that lack of technical competency of the students, and teacher make difficulties to innovative instructional practices and it also leads to a barrier for making good and quality video, audio, and learning materials. A study conducted by Kamal, A.A. et al. (2020) indicated there are many students say they are felt uncomfortable to taking an examination through online mode because of unjustified action like cheating, unwanted discussion, etc. (Arkorful & Abaidoo, 2015). Another important challenge of pedagogy to lack of management of online classes, lack of providing valuable feedback, and lack of emotional attachment during the instruction, etc. (Parkes et al., 2014). Pedagogical challenges is a lack of two-way interaction between students and teachers due to the reason for technical challenges (Mishra, L. et al. 2020). One study revealed that due to the lack of digital competency in the instructor, many instructors was not capable to deliver high quality of instruction to the learners (Adedoyin, O.B., & Soykan, E. 2020).

3. Financial challenges: India is a developing country. Here the majority of the population belongs to low economic status, and average economic status. For continuing the online mode learning there are many devices are needed like, smartphone/laptop, modem, internet connectivity, electricity etc. which are very costly. So, there are many families that are faced with economic crises due to continuing their children's educational fees like the cost of a smartphone, heavy internet bill, etc. (Fishbane and Tomer 2020). Another side, due to the COVID-19 pandemic there are many people jobless, and their family income is also zero. So, it is the significant challenges for parents to continuing their child's education through online mode.

4. Behavioural challenges: Behavioural challenges refer to negative attitudes towards adopting new modes of learning and their negative impact on the students. A study also revealed that online lectures will lead to laziness and a negative effect on performance, and it also hampered the social relationship (Khalil, R. et al. 2020). Another study also revealed that learning through an online mode the student faced several challenges like, imbalance of socioemotional relationships, difficulty to adjust everyday activities at home (UNESCO IESALC, 2020). Another study shows that 75% of students say long time used of smartphones for online learning leads to different types of eye-related issues, like to eye strain, euphoria, and headache, etc. It also affects daily life like decrease outdoor activities which lead to physical health, communication skills due to social isolation (Shetty, S. et al., 2020).

5. Digital Divide: While e-education is a privilege for the students from an upper and middle class, it has proved to be a nuisance for students from the lower middle class and people living below the poverty line. Many poor students who don't have access to e-resources (computers, laptops, internet connectivity) shall not be able to attend classes from home.

6. Commercialisation of Education: With online education becoming a norm in the post-pandemic era, there is a significant possibility of corporate houses, technology firms and educational institutions working much more closely together.

Though this may have a big positive effect on the education sector, it may further aggravate the ongoing commercialisation of the education sector and exclude the self-dependent tutors.

7. Poor network connectivity: Since the network connection is not good at every place the students are required to step out of their houses in order to get mobile signal which is perilous as it unnecessarily increases the chances of coming in contact with more people thereby increasing the probability of contracting Covid-19. **8. High Data Consumption**-If an online class via Google Meet, Zoom etc. is conducted the data consumed is high and given the daily data limit, it becomes difficult even for the students who have the access to internet to overcome this issue as their data gets exhausted by online classes itself so there is hardly any scope left for completing the assignments and research using online resources.

9. Multiple users for single device-Although, a household might have access to internet but if there are more than one student and the device is required to be shared then it becomes more problematic given the data consumption rate, overlapping of timings of online classes etc.

10. Financial Limitations-There are students who come from economically weak background for whom it is not always to open to get their phones recharged given the lockdown conditions and financial strain.

11. Low Attendance- When online classes are conducted due to the problems faced the attendance of students becomes very low and only a handful of students can participate in online classes.

12. Lack of Authentic Resources for Assignments & Research-As far as assignments, research/term-papers are concerned, it becomes a herculean task for the students to work on their papers as Wikipedia, Google etc. are not perse sufficient for an authentic, qualitative and reliable work. Hence, development of more e-libraries with free membership or at a nominal cost must be provided to the student community for facilitating their studies.

13. Lack of Trained Teachers for imparting online education- Not all teachers are well equipped for imparting online education and given the low internet access rates & the ability to use it limits the scope of online teaching-learning process. Even training of teachers in this regard needs to be carried online at present which is not feasible for many teachers due to the lack of their technological skills.

14. Lack of communication with every student-It is not possible for the teachers to communicate with every student personally, unlike in physical classroom which atleast provides an opportunity to feel the physical presence of every student.

15. Lack of Check and Balance- Maintenance of discipline is vital in learning process and one cannot take a lenient view of education. Online platform provides less opportunity for check and balance on students unlike in classroom teaching which ensures comparatively higher level of discipline& understanding. Further, in classrooms by looking at a student, a teacher can determine whether a student is able to pay attention and understand what is being taught in the class, however, virtual teaching limits such ability as it is not feasible to watch every student given the screen sharing and network issues. Despite being present in online class, most of the times students tend to turn off their camera and mic due to which it is not practicable to determine whether a student is actually paying attention in the online class or not, or has merely joined for getting attendance.

16. Lack of Learning Ambience-Physically attending schools, colleges etc. every day is a boon as it provides a positive learning ambience to students and at the same time students can interact with their class fellows, friends, teachers, staffs, seniors, juniors etc. Lunch hours & recess are fun as students can hangout in the canteens with peers who are an integral part of their lives. Such memories of a student's life are cherished forever but now the scenario has entirely changed everything has shifted online with schools and colleges being shut down which has confined the students to a single screen at their homes which can never substitute the positive ambience of educational institutes.

17. Excess Screen Time-With the shift of learning from classrooms to virtual screens, the time spent by the students on screen has increased which can grossly affect their health. Report published by Organization for Economic Co-operation & Development (OECD) on *Impacts of Technology use of Children: Exploring Literature on the Brain, Cognition & Wellbeing,* reveals that increased screen time is linked to risks such as radio frequency damage, musculoskeletal problems, eyestrain, sleep disturbances and can also cause stress. Hence, regulation of Screen time is quintessential and needs to be balanced cautiously while scheduling and structuring virtual classes.

18. **Depleting Mental Health**-The pandemic has increased mental health issues especially among students; who are in the final year of their college or who have to appear for board exams the coming year or the ones having no access to resources to continue their education through online mode.

19. **Impact on Socialization**- Due to social/physical distancing norms there is a probability that students might get used to being isolated and lose their values of sharing space with fellow classmates.

20. **Increased Risk of Cyber Crimes**- Greater the cyber engagement more are the risks of cyber crimes which can affect students as they are the vulnerable ones and can easily fall prey to the evil motives of such criminals.

21. **Online Examination**-Given the limitations of virtual classrooms marking the students on the basis of online examination is not an ideal option as there is every likelihood of cheating as for monitoring the students during examination would mean to have constant internet connection, computer with web camera etc. which are available to merely a handful of students. Hence, online examination cannot be a fair and feasible alternative at present.

22. **Socio-economic Challenges:** The socio-economic challenges that we undergo today affect the marginalized students and families the most. Many students don't have access to home learning and parent supporting environment and are at most disadvantaged by closure of schools. Many parents have lost jobs; many parents face difficulties to make both ends meet, and many parents are struggling to pay their rent. Therefore, the pandemic affected every student on the earth, but not all affected equally. UNESCO Director-General Audrey Azoulay noted that "We now see that online distance learning cannot be the sole solution, as it tends to exacerbate already existing inequalities that are partly leveled in school settings. This will be of interest to this Commission whose task is rethinking the future of education, including appropriate articulation between distance and classroom learning".

23. **Access to Technology:** The sudden shift from F2F to online virtual classrooms makes all happy but there is a hidden side that blooms the efforts put in. Many students reside in remote areas and live in poverty.

They don't have access to technology that needs electronic gadgets like mobile phones, laptops, the internet, digital skills, etc. The students become anxious, frustrated, and worried about missing the important classes pushing them far behind those students who live in urban areas with access to technology.

24. Internet Connectivity: with the given facts above, the people living in remote areas don't get uninterrupted electricity, internet connectivity, and no signals for mobile networks all contribute to students' damage to their course learning. In an interview with the New York Times, Gordon (2020) estimated that 30 to 40 percent of families lack a suitable device or Internet access.

25. Content: The current situation has compelled authorities to assign teachers to undertake remote and virtual classes at short notice. This made teachers perplexed and upset to attend to the content preparation to the level and course for the students. The teaching became cumbersome and monotonous without the activities arousing students' interest to partake. It created chaos and anxiety in students who couldn't comprehend the contents taught and makes them scared of the topics.

26. Learning Time: The teacher finds difficult to make a balance among allocated time, instructional, engaged and academic time (Wong & Wong,1998) because the students' lack of motivation in teacher instruction and learning, participation and involvement in a given task and time teachers can feel and prove that students have learned the content effectively. Persistent absenteeism during good times may even become worse now, with lessons being conducted remotely, more students are missing class- not logging on, not checking in, or not completing activities or assignments.

27. Paucity of Funds: James Walker et al (2020) found that the researchers have undermined their confidence in applying for grants that are not focused on Covid-19 and are concerned that the extreme focus on the pandemic would mean less funding and attention for some of the other major challenges humanity faces. It doesn't pay heed to the major concerns the teachers and students face in undertaking remote and virtual classes on digital platforms. Secondly, the teachers and researchers get very little time to devote to research. The abrupt shift to online teaching and learning consume an increased amount of time being devoted to teaching, assessment, and management, to ensure quality of education for the students. The survey concludes that the time required catering students' needs means less time given to research activities. Around 76% of teachers felt online teaching was a lot more time-consuming to prepare, while about 40 % found online evaluation also took up more time. It also underscores the inequalities, with junior teachers seeing a 5% more rise in time devoted to teaching and assessment than their senior teachers who have been able to devote time to research. This could impact on their career progression.

28. Cumbersome Schedule: Both IT staff and teachers have been stretched by a sudden change to online teaching making multiple changes to their work habits, uploading their teaching materials online, and get to digital skills to online lecturing. Teachers sometimes record many videos for use in one or two classes, and evaluating each student's assignments and uploading feedback. Many people work tirelessly, around the clock to provide training to teachers on how to use digital platforms for synchronous teaching and learning. Teachers have to prepare in-class activities, quizzes, assignments, group discussions, and update presentations to make more informative and interesting because a few learning experiences cannot be replicated digitally.

29. Learners' Pre-existing Knowledge: The last semester witnessed virtual classes undertaken remotely by teachers by arresting and challenging the imagination based on students existing subject knowledge, which would be unknown for the new students. Teachers and students would need time and special attention to tune to new topics. Teachers should adapt and be flexible in their approach in online teaching. It throws a great challenge for the teachers to evolve their plans, select content wisely to fulfill students' needs.

30. Poor Online Engagement: The consistent engagement of students in virtual classes is very critical and results in an increase in dropout rates. The students usually develop social relationships and have peer-to-peer interactions in schools. This is about learning to be a good human being, a citizen, and developing social skills. Teacher s and parents should stay connected with the students by any means. These tough, terrible, and difficult situations develop socio-emotional skills and learn more about their own capabilities and strengths. Parents and family roles also become extremely crucial to guide and counsel their wards. Social media, TV, and SMS messages can be used to provide tips and advice to parents on how to better communicate, handle, and support their children graciously.

31. Learning Outcomes not Achieved: Many studies pointed out that online learning did not affect student learning outcomes significantly.

Providing guidance online for learning for many students seems less successful than does use such means with individual learners. It commonly influences the way students interact, but not the total they learn. Even video or online quizzes, tests, and assignments do not appear to influence the total that students learn in online classes. The research does not support the use of some frequently recommended online learning practices.

32. No Concrete Final Assessment and Evaluation: The switching over to online posted many challenges to assess and evaluate students' subject learning. The institutions could not conduct final exams giving more weight to weekly assignments and less weight to mass final exams. But practical applications of knowledge learned, such as laboratory-based classes in science, have also been canceled and final marks calculated on the bases of current semester assignments and previous semester final marks. This action has reduced the negative impact of this pandemic on students to get back on a path of faster improvement in learning.

Challenges from the student's point of view

Online classes are not as easy as it seems .It involves many factors which make it effective. It is a new concept which helps students to learn and acquire knowledge through online mode. Though it was a new concept for both teachers and students, no one knew about it effectiveness but managed somehow a step ahead to engage students in studies and to get connected with their studies. "The pandemic is going to cause the greatest disruption to education opportunity that the world has experienced in at least a century" as stated by Fernando M. Reimers, Ford foundation Professor, Harvard Graduate School of Education.No one is prepared for this situation and the trend of online classes. Students have different perspective to online learning. For some it is of great help and but some are taking it casually. It mostly depends on students to grab from whatever area it comes through.

- **Lack of proper mobile phones to access internet**: As we all know the fact that India has a large number of people, (that is 25.7%, according to RBI) who are below poverty line cannot afford handsets which can access internet facility. So online classes for them is like impossible.
- **Internet speed**: Internet speed is not same everywhere. At some places, there is a very less signal and at some place it is almost zero. So it is difficult to get connected throughout online class session.

- **Communication barrier**: It becomes chaotic when children speak at same time during online class, no one is audible at that time and there is a chance to miss some of the important conversation.
- **Lack of interest**: Spending too much time on phone that too on studies, sometimes lead to dullness, tiredness. Due to which students loss their interest in studies.
- **Spending too much time on phone**: As classes are going online so for this, students have to spend maximum time on phone which proves to be hazardous for their eyesight which is a major concern for most of the parents.
- **Lack of study material**: Everyone was clueless that all of sudden, world will be at hold because of lockdown. Leaving everyone to leave their hostels, places as it is without any preparations. Students left their places and ran towards their home without books and other study material which disturbed their preparations.
- **Many health issues**: Due to their long sitting on phone or computer leads to many health issues, some may face backaches, depression, anxiety etc, which is a serious threat for their well being.
- **Shyness in clearing doubts**: Online classes are going in a group, where the students with average intelligence may lack behind in comparison to other students of their class. They can feel shy to clear doubts and sometimes let the things go away, which is not a good sign for their mental development.

Challenges faced by teachers to make teaching effective and fruitful

We cannot deny the fact that every teacher despite being at home is giving his best to make students learn and understand well during online classes. Classroom teaching is different to that of online teaching. In classroom's, teacher can note the expressions of his/her students about the clarity of thoughts where in online mode, a teacher just expect that what he/she delivers is making an impact on students. Teaching through online mode is putting a lot of pressure on Teacher as they have to give their best so that students can learn from it. Teachers are using every possible means and methods to make teaching effective but for fruitful and effective results. Teaching-learning process goes hand in hand. It needs the contribution from both the teacher and the student. Major responsibility is on the heads of teachers as they will be questioned. Some of the challenges and struggles which teachers are facing during COVID-19 period are discussed below here:

- **Role of teachers diversified**: In this time of pandemic COVID-19, everyone is at home. Doing everything themselves, which increased their daily routine burden. Therefore, it is getting difficult to make teaching plans, lessons being at home with a very less material available .But still teachers are doing quite well .Here role of teachers multiplied by many times as compare to classroom teaching.

- **Lack of attentiveness on part of students**: Online mode of classes is a blessing for the serious learners but some of the students mocked at it and make fun of it which disturbs overall class environment. It becomes difficult for the teachers to deliver their lecture that too in restrained time.

- **Preparing lesson plans and videos**: During this period of pandemic, teachers came up with different pattern of lesson plans. They also prepared videos, audios and also other kind of material which help the students to learn and understand things easily.

- **Multiple responsibilities**: Teachers not only making students learn new things but also playing the role of a guide for the students. Teacher fraternity has played a wonderful as well as crucial role in this tough time. They guide the students to stay indoors and safe but also to engage them in a better possible way. They also motivated the students to be calm and patient and to learn their own.

- **Mental trauma**: Every teacher wants their children to learn the best things and they are making best efforts to solve every single problem of their students. For this they are making best plans to encounter the hurdles, but still are in dilemma about the student's mental level. So this procedure is full of trauma for the teachers at this crucial stage.

- **Imparting knowledge through online mode is not less than a war without a weapon**: It would not be wrong if it is said that teachers are playing a blind role at hitting the target, because they exactly don't know where to hit .which means that they don't know the real worth of what students learned through their online classes. They just move ahead on the basis of assumptions.

- **Facing indiscipline**: Like two sides of the coin. Online leaning too has different aspects to it. In this where teachers aims at clearing doubts and completing the syllabus, on other hand, students are not showing their concerns. It has been observed that during the online classes, some were lying on beds and is found sleeping, which is not acceptable and are creating indiscipline. Some also make remarks with fake identities and creating nuisance.

- **Deal with parents as well as students**: During online classes, parents also have direct contact with the teachers. They also try to judge the performance of teachers which sometimes lead to insecurity and complex among the teachers.
- Adaptability-Adapting to technology took time for the teachers had to learn themselves as they were not used to such technologies. They learned from the You tube video or their own elder kids and then teach. There were many who had no knowledge about MS Word and PowerPoint and whenever some technical issued emerged they would find difficulty solving it. They faced many difficulties with live classes, usage of appropriate icons, MS Office, communication related apps and websites, browsing, checking. Not only this the environment immediately changed from traditional base education to commuter based one.
- Figuring out online class etiquette took some time- learning the tools to conduct the class, was only one step. The students would not mute themselves and so many noises would come from the background.
- Parents hovering around during class became an issue- one of the biggest issues, though, is that parents also have access to these classes. There were multiple memes of parents attending classes and taking notes instead of the children, which prompted the institutions to send out circulars against these behaviors. Some parents began commenting on the quality of teaching, following which a video titled "Parents! Please be patient with teachers who are starting online classes" came up on social media to address parents and how it makes teaching difficult for teachers.
- Maintaining discipline was tough-students would log in mute themselves and turn the videos off and do other stuff. Screen sharing would be hampered.
- Engaging students and lack of motivation in students- one of the common problems in online learning modules is that students become more passive than active participants. This is a knowledge they are getting but not essentially registering, to apply practically in real-world situations. As students moved towards online learning from traditional classrooms, it became difficult for teachers to adjust to a new learning

platform. Teaching online did not influence or engage students and it was a very big challenge.

- There was a lack of appropriate devices such as graphics tablets and webcams for conducting them. Secondly lack of adequate internet bandwidth. Thirdly, the teacher had bring their own device and software, which meant that in order to ensure the quality of education that was to imparted, the teacher had to invest their own personal money to create that ambience through online teaching. Also, the copyrighted material that could be easily dispersed to all students.

- The situation is worse for those from the remote areas, non-urban areas. Highlighting India's digital divide, poor connectivity and lack of smart gadgets provide another hassle. problem of live for virtual learning, blurred videos, cracking voices, downloading all were a problem.

- Assessment- it is the most important part of the online teaching for students as well as teachers. So, whenever there are assignments or projects, teachers faced a lot of question from the students, expectation and performance also differed. As the students experienced less homework, less assignments and lack of examination at times then assessing them was difficult. Not only this making and checking assignments was also a bit of a problem for the teachers.

- Fear of cheating- there is always the fear of cheating by the student. As there is no one to watch them they can do it.

- Course content- it was designed with respect to traditional classroom. Due to the shift it needs to be redesigned.

- Time consumption in developing content-earlier the teacher came to the class and used to start with the teaching but when the things moved completely online they had to spend hours developing presentations and video recordings. The hours going up and the salary getting halved was a challenge that was foreseen.

- Managing collaboration online- collaboration is a key soft skill that a student would acquire during their school time. This can be achieved through various team activities that are quite common and easy to do so in a physical classroom setting, where a teacher can monitor it in real time, and give constructive feedback at every stage dynamically. The online course cannot fit for everyone.

- The roadblock- while teachers are striving to adapt to the new form of teaching by equipping themselves with technical skills, they are sadly confronted with the shenanigans of students who are changing IDs to post offensive remarks, disrupting classes by sharing memes, sleeping in class, morphing teachers pictures, and so on.

- Role of the authorities- classroom management might be a teacher's responsibility but the management's active role in it will strengthen the teacher's confidence to play their role with ease. A framework of behavior and discipline should be designed. Serious action should be taken against the offenders.

Steps to be taken

- **Online Education as a common good:** The Centre and the state governments should start making access to technology universal and more feasible in the public education system.
- **Expansion in the scope of Right to Education:** The definition of the right to education needs to expand and promote online education so that it addresses the importance of connectivity and access to knowledge and information.
- **Valuing teaching profession:** Digital innovation provides a remarkable opportunity for the democratisation of education.
- **Protection of the social spaces provided by education institutions:** Traditional classroom organization must give way to online education. However, school or education as a social space (whereby a student not just learns the academic knowledge but many social skills also) is indispensable.
- **Ensuring scientific literacy within the curriculum:** This is the right time for deep reflection on curriculum, particularly as a society still struggles against superstitions and actively fights misinformation.

Online learning is here to stay

An immediate and effective response to the crisis was to go digital. Developing robust online platforms has become necessary to offer continuity in learning. Yet in a developing country like India with vast disparity in socio-economic backgrounds of students and the quality of educational institutions, the shift has not been easy. The digital divide has been further widening the gap, and needs urgent attention from both public and private sector players as the crisis continues. Good teachers, refreshed curricula and effective tools will ensure students stay involved and active in the learning process.

More Indian students will stay home in India

Lakhs of Indian students have increasingly chosen to pursue higher education abroad. As per reports, India is the second-largest source of international students in the world. This usual exodus is likely to transform—at least in the immediate few years—to an influx into Indian institutions, given travel restrictions and health risks. This means that crores of rupees and resources spent in foreign education could potentially be retained in the country, as more students look towards options at home. While international institutions might bear the brunt of the change, it is a remarkable opportunity for India to enhance its capacities and offer quality education at par with global standards.

Sources and Importance of E-learning and E-teaching.

The teaching fraternity with the use of many e teaching or e learning applications such as Google class room, Zoom, Easy Class, Go To Meeting, Remind, Slack and many others have been adopted to reach the students as far as possible. Now the bigger challenge was to select an application among the ocean of applications available on the internet catering to every ones needs with low data consumption and better stability during the

The effects of global economy:

The economy has taken a severe hit, and its ripples can be felt in the education sector as well. While many students will chart alternative paths, the pandemic is also leaving others in limbo. As unemployment is predicted to increase and the financial capacity of Indian homes comes under stress, the country can expect a drop in enrolments and challenges with tuition fees. Public institutions too, may be under threat of reduced funding. On the flipside, the pandemic could also prompt reform in fee structures and creation of more cost-effective programmes.

New trends in teaching & learning will emerge in Higher Education:

Beyond the top band of institutional excellence with private universities setting best practices, Indian academia has been in need of transformation, long before the onset of the pandemic. There is an opportunity to rethink the traditional education system now.

Digital learning is leading the charge as a mainstay, and many new trends are picking up momentum across the globe. Multidisciplinary and modular pedagogy that afford transferable skills and customised learning will succeed. Post-pandemic times could see a blend of e-learning and mainstream face-to-face teaching with a boost from traditional universities and the ed-tech sector.

A call for greater global collaboration between students, academia & industry:

Opportunities for student mobility and practical exposure through exchange programmes, internships, participation in conferences, and more could likely be off the table for some time. Innovative new forms of collaboration and alternative paradigms are needed to drive learning, research and teaching. Sharing of knowledge between institutions globally through joint-teaching, virtual guest lectures, etc. could give students an enriched global perspective in these difficult times.

As education systems deal with this crisis, we should also think of how we can build up our strength, with an improved sense of responsibility and with compassion, adaptability, flexibility, and sense of exigency of the need to shut the gap in opportunities and assuring that students across have the same chances for quality education.

6.3. Objective 3: To study the effect of online mode of education on the students of Higher Education with respect to their economical background.

Data analysis has been done on the basis of actual data received from respondents through questionnaire technique. Simple percentage distribution was estimated to assess the time spent at home, communication tools, assignment related problem and educational problems related to study due to the lockdown.

Table 1: STUDENTS IN SEMESTER WISE (n=100)

Sr. No.	Details	Frequency(n)	Percentage (%)
01	Semester-I	00	00
02	Semester-II	40	40
03	Semester-III	00	00
04	Semester-IV	60	60

Interpretation: Table 1 shows that, semester I & III under graduate students don't include in this data. While 40% students are belongs to

Semester II and 60% students are semester IV.

Conclusion: Only semesters II and IV students are included in this data.

Table 2: TIME SPENT AT HOME BY RESPONDENTS (n=100)

Sr. No.	Details	Frequency(n)	Percentage (%)
01	Watching Television	16	16
02	Doing Assignment	64	64
03	Cooking	20	20

Interpretation: It is clear from table 2 that, 16% respondents are spending their time on watching television,64% are spending their time for completing assignments and 20% respondents are giving time for cooking.

Conclusion: That means maximum time is spent by respondents on doing assignments.

Table 3: GADGETS FOR ATTENDING ONLINE CLASSES

Sr. No.	Details	Frequency	Percentage (%)
01	Computer	2	2
02	Laptop	6	6
03	Mobile phone (Android)	90	90
04	Mobile phone (Without Android)	2	2

Interpretation: It is observed that, 2% respondents have computer at home, 6% having laptops, 92% having mobile phone and 2% respondents having mobile phone without android. Most of the respondents (90%) used android mobile for attending e-learning and another of students used laptops or computer for e-learning purposes.

Conclusion: Maximum respondents having android mobile phone.

Table 4: WHETHER MOBILE PHONE IS GOOD EDUCATIONAL RESOURCE

Strongly disagree		Neutral		Agree		Strongly agree		Disagree	
Responde nts	%	Responde nts	%	Responde nts	%	Responde nts	%	Responde nts	%
06	06	24	24	44	44	24	24	02	02

Interpretation: whether mobile phone is good educational resource such question was asked respondents responses to this sentence such as 06% strongly disagree, 24% neutral, 44% agree, 24% strongly agree and 02% are disagree.

Conclusion: That means 44% respondents are agree that mobile phone is good educational resource.

Table 5: ASSIGNMENT COMPLETION (n=100)

Sr. No.	Details	Frequency(n)	Percentage (%)
01	Completed on the basis of classroom teaching	52	52
02	Completed by own	38	38
03	Not completed	10	10

Interpretation: Table No 05 show that, 52 % respondents completed their assignments on the basis of classroom teaching, 38% assignments completed by own, while 10% respondents do not completed their assignments.

Conclusion: That means maximum 52% respondents completed their assignments on the basis of classroom teaching.

Table 6: EDUCATIONAL PROBLEMS FACED AT HOME

Sr. No.	Details	Frequency	Percentage (%)
01	Concept not cleared from notes	60	60
02	Parents are unable to help	38	38
03	find any difficulties could not solved	44	44
04	Lack of teachers guidance	50	50

Interpretation: If you observed table 6 it show that, 60% respondents do not have cleared concept from notes, 38% respondents' parents are unable to help, 44% respondents having educational difficulty at home and 50% respondents have lack of teacher's guidance.

Table 7: DAILY TIME SPENT BY RESPONDENTS DURING LOCKDOWN PERIOD

Items	Study				Cooking				Singing				Social media			
Hrs	2hrs	3hrs	4hrs	5hrs	2hrs	3hrs	4hrs	5hrs	2hrs	3hrs	4hrs	5hrs	2hrs	3hrs	4hrs	5hrs
respondents	46	24	14	16	62	10	06	02	26	04	02	00	16	34	20	18
%	46	24	14	16	62	10	06	02	26	04	02	00	16	34	20	18

Interpretation: If we observed table 7 it show that, 46% ,24%, 14% and 16% respondents give time for study purpose such as 2hrs, 3hrs, 4hrs and 5hrs. For cooking 62%, 10%, 06% and 2% respondents spent their time such as 2hrs, 3hrs, 4hrs and 5hrs. And 16%, 34%, 20% and 18% respondents spent their time on social media such as 2hrs, 3hrs, 4hrs and 5hrs.

Conclusion: It is clear that maximum respondents are spent their time on social media and study during lockdown period.

Respondent Views on Education related to Present Scenario

Many teachers and students have been suffered due to the close education institution. As there is no option to continuation of the classes without the help of digital education some of the universities have been have already begun preparing lesson plans to deliver online teaching to their students.

Table 8: Student and Teacher Views on Study

Category	Online Education	Face to Face Education	Overall Condition Of study
Student Views	32	68	worst
Teacher Views	27	73	worst

Source: Primary Data, 2020

In this Pandemic situation Digital education is the only way to continue studies. But in a developing country like India, every student cannot afford to conduct their studies through a digital platform. As this kind of crisis student and teachers has no option without accepting online platform but only 32 percentage of students and 27 percentage of teachers are support this online education. According to them due to the lockdown the total condition of education was collapsed.

Table 9: Digital Platform Used by Respondent

Digital Platform	Yes	No	Maybe
(Using E-library, whatsapp, googlemeet, swayam, email, smart board etc.)	49%	21%	30%

Source: Primary Data, 2020

Above table represent that near about 49 percentage of respondent are using the digital platform like E Library,Whatsupp,Email,Smart Phone erc.On the other side 21 percent of respondent are unable to use any of this for there learning purpose as they are unable to access this ,lack of financial and lack of institutional support.(Nagar.S,2020)

Impact of Examination System and Evaluation Process

The education sector is also going through pan world basis as the COVID-19. (Mitra .A, 2020). All the examination of school, colleges, university as well as entrance exam and recruitment exam have been cancelled due to the outbreak of covid 19. (MHRD,2020). The ongoing higher secondary examination stopped due to this and the government of west Bengal decided to evaluated their result on the basis of highest marks which a student getting of the other subject which was taken. On the other sight the mid semester students are promoted as there are no facilities to take the online examination. (Govt. Of West Bengal, 2020)

Table 10: Information about the Examination

Name of the Exam		Status	Evaluation
Secondary		Complete	Going on
Higher Secondary		Incomplete	Based on Highest marks in one subject
Graduation	Mid Semester	Not Taken	Promoted for next semester
	End Semester	Yet not Decided	
Post-Graduation	Mid Semester	Not Taken	Promoted for next semester
	End Semester	Yet not Decided	
Entrance Exam		Not Decided	
Recruitment Exam		Not Decided	

Source: Govt. Of West Bengal, 2020

Future Prospectus of Education

There of many students in the educational institutions today, a generation that has grown up in a truly globalized world. This generation, the oldest of whom are now 25 years old, is likely to be reflecting on their education as a result of a truly global pandemic, with many facing cancelled exams, sporting events and even graduation. Though E learning is one of the major solutions to combat with that but due to this effect may the generation will suffer several day. Many of the students cannot afford studying on internet during this lockdown period. And the traditional way of teaching and learning process was more convenient.

Table 11: For Quality of Future Education

Choice of respondent based on facilities provided by institutions, (1=best ,2=good,3=Moderate,4=bad)				
Parameters	1	2	3	4
E learning infrastructure provided by educational institution	0	1	12	87
Student achievement	1	3	17	79
Quality Of education	0	3.2	15	81.8
Teaching Learning process	0	2	16	82
Student accessibilities	2	1	23	74

Source: Primary survey, 2020

Above table define the rank wise categorization the present condition of education provide by them. Most of the student chosen the worst condition of education due to the outbreak of corona its clearly define that it may effect their future education as well as career .Online platform is not suitable for the country like India as there are 64 percent of people are under below the poverty line.

Impact of Students

COVID-19 impacts on education negatively particularly to the poor and rural section of the society. Because poor and rural people are not getting proper benefits of online classes due to slow network or not having smart phone, internet connection and financial crisis. Higher secondary students and even those in graduation and rest are suffering. Online classes are not available for all as universities and colleges have not enough infrastructures to to provide them a proper and fruitful education. Even it's also effect their mental health due to this student is psychologically not stable to learn in a proper manner.

Table 12: Status of Network Connectivity

Category	Percentage of Respondent
High speed Broadband connection used	39
E-instrument used	59
Institutional free resource accessibilities	89
High Network connection	41
No Network Connection	25

Source: Primary Survey, 2020

Above table represent the status of network connectivity uses by the Respondent. Only 41 percent of people get high speed connectivity though they also faced many difficulties.89 percent respondent are using E-resources which provided by the institution. According to them the quality of E-resources are not suitable as follows the syllabus provided by the different universities.It is difficult to understand the topics properly by providing only notes or online class.Internet connection problems may occur during the classes, strong internet connection is costly during the lockdown period.(Mitra.A,2020).

Perception of students about online learning: Learners become very happy because they are liberal to utilize the time absolutely. As they have lot of time as they do not have to attend the class physically. It saves extra time which they have to spend during traditional class. At the very beginning of online learning during lockdown, a large part of students face difficulty to access online class but later they are able to adapt the it easily. Online learning made the learners alone. They did not meet their peers and the teachers face to face. They are compelled to it because they have to save themselves from corona virus affection. The online learning makes it fruitful.

Languages of delivery of online learning should be comprehensible. It means that priority should be given to the local or regional language so that learners from different languages can understand it without any effort.

Learners, who have not a little knowledge of technology, have become unhappy and frustrated about online learning. They did not adjust themselves with online learning. Online learning is very effective for women and physically challenged learners who face difficulty to attend the traditional class due to some unavoidable reasons. Some students have failed to manage the schedule time to attend the online class for a lot of valid reasons. Learners are requesting to upload all the recording classes for future references so that they would be beneficial to revisit the class. Consequently, they have got the chance to clear their doubts and concept.

Students in the Pandemic Scenario

Most schools and colleges have been focusing on preparing and improving the infrastructure to make it more responsive to the needs of students. A number of factors in the present situation are making possible, what for decades had only been imaginable, the widespread provision of free, online learning, technology-based resources and Educational Resource materials, irrespective of a student's financial or social status, geographic location, or their ability to access institutional facilities. However there are barriers and hindrances to learning associated with current online learning scenario that has to be dealt with.

One important factor influencing teaching learning is Students' accessibility to knowledge and information through cable network, television, radio, internet, digital media, and social media such as Facebook, Twitter, What's app, Instagram, Linkedin, you tube. Infants at a very early age get used to interacting with touchscreen phones. This early exposure to multisensory devices mayor may not have a positive impact on a child's readiness to learn. Moreover without a meaningful regulation and supervision from a teacher, children's communication with smart phone may become unsafe as they have the potential to have a negative impact on the growing child. Thus knowledge to be propagated through technology in a healthy manner should be channelized meaningfully and appropriately.

Learning is the neuro-biological process that takes place in the brain. It functions through a genetically fixed networking of neurons. The human brain constitutes 1. Neuron: Basic unit of brain. Human brain contains 1010 (ten thousand million) neurons. 2. Dendrites: Acting as an input channel. 3. Axon: Acting as output channel of neuron. 4. Synapse: Axon terminates in a specific contact called synapse. When axon hit synapse, synapse releases chemicals (neurotransmitters) across the gap. These chemicals diffuse across the gap and chemically activate gates on the dendrites which permits charged ions to flow when opened. Increasing number of ions flow and learning to take place when more gates open on the dendrite. Learning will be enhanced if there is an increase in number of inputs.

New technologies the Internet, the World Wide Web, laptops, desktop computers, interactive whiteboards, tablets and smart phones have emerged for dissemination of knowledge. A well modified technological integration should be the driving force behind this extensive Innovation that will allow schools and colleges to engage in sustainable methods to generate possibilities for a radically different and improved quality of instruction.Effort should be made to rethink and redesign the educational systems and processes based on technology to provide quality education for all. It is an important aspect of a broader educational objective to provide Education for All and experiment proactively with new and emerging online learning strategy.

Online Learning in this present pandemic scenario represents a challenge as well as opportunities for the future functioning of the academic institution. It has the potential to offer greater openness, efficiency and cost-effectiveness in education. It can be characterized as being the harbinger of 'new income generation opportunities and unparalleled reach for all the learners', Educational institutions in rural and urban areas can play a significant role in these turbulent times by adapting effective practice according to new contexts while at the same time understanding how digital technologies can best support teaching and meaningful, authentic learning. Learning which is an active process of communication, creation and distribution and dissemination of knowledge will remain valid if it is connected through digital technologies.

Pedagogical basis for Effective Technology Integration

Learning is an active process in which a relationship is established between the learner, the learning experiences and the newly acquired information.New knowledge is fabricated and founded on children's past knowledge and experience. "Education is the process of living through a continuous reconstruction of experiences," John Dewey's (1938). Instead of passively absorbing the new information the learner makes an attempt to establish a relationship between new information and previously acquired knowledge. Participation and interaction of students for reconstruction of knowledge is important.Teachers should prepare the lessons on the basis of past learning and make attempt to activate prior knowledge as often as possible to encourage participation of students in the learning process.Discussion within the classroom context leads to enhancement of Learning experiences and a better understanding of new content knowledge. Contextualizing new content information within a meaningful framework grounds the learning experience for students by adding numerous options for connecting prior knowledge to new knowledge.

Constructivist learning theory suggests that it is through discussion that knowledge and meaning are constructed. To practice and deepen newly acquired content information, learners should engage in learning tasks that allow them to talk about new information, reflect on that information, and engage in collaborative problem-solving or investigative tasks in which that new information is applied (Vygotsky, 1978).The Cognitive Constructivism of Piaget considered learners as a little scientist and discoverers of knowledge, capable of constructing an understanding of the world but Vygotsky's Social Constructivism developed from Piaget's ideas put emphasis on social interaction in learning and development.

Learners learn better with the help of visual presentation, pictorial depictions and illustrative words.Bloom (1956) classified educational objectives into three main domains; cognitive, affective and psychomotor. ICT use in classrooms helps transmitting knowledge through visual connotation, sounds, and written words thereby giving opportunities for innovative and collaborative learning.Learning environments with proper integration of technologies and enhanced multisensory interaction, expression and representation of knowledge, discussion and feedback, expands students' attention capacity and perception skills and enhances learning.

6.4.Objective 4: To examine the initiatives taken by the Government of India to keep continue the higher education during pandemic.

During COVID-19 pandemic, Ministry of Education has held several initiatives along with various State Governments to promote online education and studies doesn't get hamper due to lockdown. To ensure that there is no break in the education during pandemic and students get full-access to classes like before, Ministry of Human Resource Development advises students to carry on with their studies using the online learning platforms. The online learning platforms help the students not only to get full access to the study material but also allow them to engage in online classes and interact with the teachers like the traditional classroom setting.

Indian government has taken promptly concoction against the widely spreading of novel corona virus. It has adopted a number of preventive measures. All the educational institutions of whole country have been announced to lock down for an uncertain time by the nation. According to the country-wide lock down, all levels of institutions have postponed their education related activities completely. After July 31st almost all the states have decided to monitor the ensuring not to encumbering the academic activities of schools, colleges and universities for the sake of lock down period. Educational institutions have been dictated to maintain their academic works and class through online learning mode. It was best time to use technology effectively. It has accepted an active part in the lock down period to continue the study and work staying at home. MHRD has introduced several arrangements to maintain the academic activities with along online portals and educational channels through direct to home TV and radio has acted as an active educational online learning tool for students to set their academic goals. Both teacher and student are accomplishing the fruitful usage of popular social media like Facebook live, zoom, Google-meet, telegram, you-tube and what's-app for online teaching learning system. Ministry of education has initiated ICT and it is an absolute platform which comprised of all digital resources. Ministry of education has taken the initiatives for all level of educational system.

Role of Government in changing the situation of present Education System

In the post-pandemic world, there may be a shift in admission trends, where a lot of parents- due to lack of savings-would prefer government school over private. The government can use this as a good opportunity to improve public education system, and aim to make it more egalitarian. The Centre and the state governments should start making access to technology more feasible in public education system. As part of their responsibility, they can involve tech-based organisations to make e-resources accessible and available to students, especially in government and low-income private schools. A lot of teachers are made to do administrative work which often leaves them little or no time to prepare lesson plans and assessments. Besides, post the pandemic, one of the major responsibilities of these teachers would be to drive the census exercise across the country. These are some online learning platforms:

Ed Tech Start-Up in Times of Corona: Ed tech start-up is one of the most valuable tools which provide the online courses to the learners at an interval of critical situations of the country. It is suggested by UNESCO during lock down. Ed tech start up is very helpful and lucrative for students to overcome the difficult condition. The effective usage of Ed tech stat up is expected to enhance performance. It was tempting constantly to provide free courses and e-resources to the students although, the electricity and internet are still bigger challenges for villages, small cities and remote areas. Educators also encounter a lot of trouble at the time of working on it. They were confused how they used it, when they used it and how to handle it for the well-being of the students. It acts as a good instructor but cannot replace the teacher.

Diksha portal: Diksha portal is fecundated with the curriculum including text books, work sheets, video lessons and assessment for student and teacher. CBSE and NCERT have made contents for more than 250 teachers who would be able to teach in multiple languages.

E-Pathshala: NCERT has initiated a multilingual e-learning app named E-Pathshala for class i-xii. It contains the content as like diksha portal. NCERT has propagated 1886 audios, 2000 videos, 696 e-books and 504 flip books for diverse language students in this web portal.

National Repository of Open Educational Resource (NROER): It is also a multilingual resource portal for students and teachers. It is composed with books, interactive modules and videos with along STEM-based games. It has contained a vast number of 14527 files.

SWAYAM: It is specially generated for both school and higher education. It is comprised with 1900 courses covering all subjects including humanities, social science, law and management. It is exceptional for its conventional education. The main objective of SWAYAM is to fulfill the lack which the students are facing during lock down period for the sake of school closure. **SWAYAM**Study Webs of Active Learning for Young Aspiring Minds is India's MOOCs platform offering online courses on all disciplines including Engineering, Law, Management, Humanities & Social Sciences and some Professional Courses. It was launched on July 9th 2017 based on the cardinal principles of Access, Equity and Quality of NEP 2019. SWAYAM is an indigenously developed Cloud based IT platform. All the courses are interactive, made accessible through computers and mobile phones and can be accessed by Anyone, Anytime, Anywhere free of cost. Some of the National Coordinators are UGC, CEC, NPTEL, IGNOU, NCERT, AICTE

National Digital Library of India (NDL India) launched on June 19th 2018, provides a framework of virtual repository of learning resources with a single-window search facility. Learning resources, E-books, journals, audio books, question banks are made available to students. It is introduced by ministry of education govt. of India. It is a digital repository. The main aim of this repository is to collect and combine metadata. Full text index from several national and international libraries and other relevant resources are available in this library. It has been composed with text book, articles, videos, audio books, lectures, simulation, fiction, as well as other kinds learning media, user can register in it from all over the world.

Virtual Labs provides a fully interactive simulation environment to perform experiments, collect data, and answer questions to assess the understanding of the knowledge acquired. Effort is made to provide access to students living in remote areas in various disciplines of Science and Engineering.

E-Yantra enables the effective education across engineering colleges in India on embedded systems and Robotics. The training for teachers and students is imparted through workshops where participants are taught basics of embedded systems and programming. Colleges are helped to set-up Robotics labs/clubs.

FOSSEE promotes the use of well-established open source software in educational institutions through instructional material, such as spoken tutorials, documentation, such as textbook companions, awareness programmes, such as conferences, training workshops, and Internships.

SODHGANGA: Sodhganga is specially designed for the reservation of Indian thesis. It has contained those thesis and dissertations which are submitted to Indian universities. It is an open access reservoir from where users are able to read and download the full text of all the documents. It is administered by INFLIBNET center and is located in the campus of Gujarat university, Ahmedabad.

SWAYAM PRABHA: It has 32 DTH TV channels. It is broadcasting educational contents on 24*7 bases. This channel is also accessible all over the nation. It contains the same configurations like SWYAM. **SWAYAM PRABHA** provides thirty two educational channels through DTH (Direct to Home) throughout the country. It was launched on July 9th 2017 to enable continuous distribution of e-education in a cost effective and inclusive manner. Courses are based on fixed Curriculum to meet the needs of life-long learners both India and abroad.

E-PG PATHSHALA: PG students are benefited through this platform. E-books, online courses, and study material are available for students during lock down across the country. It is tremendous because the student can access these facilities besides being no internet service for the whole day.

UG–PG MOOCS: UGC initiated 100 PG courses and over 200 UG courses through SWAYAM platform. The full form of MOOC is Massive Open Online Course. It has been lunched by UGC and SWYAM portal. MOOC has been initiated by Indian government. The main aim of establishing MOOC is to enable, access, equity and quality in education sector for young aspirants learner.

E-Sodh Sindhu: It is recommended by the ministry of education in India. It is a combination of UG-INFONET, NLIST and AICTE consortium. The main objective of it is to provide e-resources for higher education. It has contained e-journal, e-journal archive, and e- books on perceptual basis. Scholarly contents are available in open access through subject portal and subject gateway.

Vidwan: Vidwan is established by INFLIBNET. It is specially formed for research scholar; expert, educational institution and policy makers. It is a valuable database .It assists to outbreak information among the experts, peers, collaborators, policy makers, and research scholars.

The National Optical Fibre Network(NOFN) now called Bharat Network aims to collect all 2,50,000 panchayats at the cost of Rs 40,000 crore. Through BharatNet, the government envisages providing a minimum of 100 Mbps bandwidth at each Gram Panchayat so that online services can be accessed by everyone, especially those in rural area. This includes e-governance, e-learning, e-health, e-commerce services. Once completed the infrastructure will be a national asset and non-discriminatory access will be a game changer in the method of service delivery and hence it must be fast tracked. The government has increased the education budget to 6% of the GDP which is a welcome move in the New National Education Policy-2020 unveiled a few months back.

2) Initiatives taken by authorities other than Government:
The pandemic has taught us a lot about adjusting to changes in new and creative ways. Government was required to provide support for digitalization to teachers as well as students by making such platforms and content available for free. One of the worst hit sectors of this pandemic is the education sector as it resulted in complete shut down of schools, college and other educational institutions, exams were cancelled, physical classes could not be taken hampering studies, practical classes, research works among many others.

i) Indian Institute of Technology Madras (IIT Madras), which is one of the best institutions of our country, is already providing an online Bachelors Degree program in Data Science and Computer Programming. The number of students admitted in this degree is around 8000+ , it's almost impossible to admit 8000+ students only in one single course in a particular institution and this is what makes this online degree different from the conventional method of learning and completing a degree. In the coming years it will be the most preferred way of learning.

ii) Indira Gandhi National Open University (IGNOU) launched Online Master's Programme in Hindi.

iii) Various Universities and Institutions organized webinars. A study conducted by GoToWebinars reported that after the lockdown the percentage of online events hosted has increased by 330% and the number of attendees are doubling with each passing month.

iv) Suggestion by UNESCO: has suggested a list of educational applications, platforms and resources to learners and educators to learn and interact during closure of educational institutions such as UNHCR, Keep Learning Going etc.

V) Action of University Grant Commission, (Use of ICT)

To combat against the corona virus outbreak, the University Grant Commission (UGC) advised to the students and teachers that to take precautionary measures, maintain social distancing and encouraged to utilize this time productively by engaging in online learning. There are many online education websites offering their content for free for education fraternity, students and teachers who are sitting at home can make full use of this learning material. The field of Higher Education has been affected by ICTs which have undoubtedly affected teaching and learning (Yusuf, 2005). There are several ICT initiatives of the MHRD, UGC and its Inter-University Centre's (IUCs) – 1. SWAYAM Online Courses, 2. UG/PG MOOCs, 3.e-PG Pathshala, 4. e-Content courseware in UG subjects, 5. Swayamprava, 6. CEC-UGC YouTube channel, 7. National Digital Library, 8. Shodhganga, 9. E-Shodh Sindhu, 10. Vidwan.Information and Library Network (INFLIBNET) and Consortium for Educational Communication (CEC), in the form of digital platforms like: Zoom App, Google class room, Team Link, Cisco WebEx, hangout and slide share, e-mail and What's App these are digital platforms can be accessed by the teachers, students, and researchers in Universities and Colleges for teaching and learning purpose. During lockdown period in India education fraternity should be used concept of "work from home" by using various online platform and being touch with the students.

Although the present Covid pandemic has negatively affected various vital sectors of the economy, including education, as mentioned above, but the outbreak of COVID has opened a ray of hope of an inevitable change to students, teachers, professors, academicians, researchers etc., to transform the so called old fashioned education system to a new technological e-learning system, with a view to make a digital India i.e, board learning process in terms of chalk, dusters, white board pens etc., to an online learning process, thereby, providing a new challenge to digitise the education sector of the country.

Importance of developing digital skills

Learners and educators have access to a universe of online educational content as well as being able to create new digital content that can support education. But the most important part here is to know the exact pathway or we can say the correct process to take the best out of this online education. And for this one should develop the digital skills as there are many things available on the internet that most of the learners and educators are unaware of. As because of the pandemic every learner and educator has an opportunity to take out some time for their daily schedule and get used to the technology which is growing up very fast worldwide. The technology sector in our country itself is a huge part of the economy and in the coming days it will contribute more and more. The jobs in the technology sector are more than any other sector in the world and because of this pandemic the technology sector is one of the sectors which got a boost. So keeping those things in mind getting accustomed to the vast field of technology is not only an option it is a necessity to cope up with the generation. So the most important thing here is to develop the digital skills and use the internet for the betterment of education. The combination of information and technology involved in digital learning makes it more practical, applicable and relatable to our life and surroundings in an interesting manner. There are multiple online platforms through which online education is being implemented which includes: Zoom, Google Meet, Skype, Facebook Live, Youtube Live, Dingtalk, Lark, Slack etc.

CHAPTER SEVEN

SUMMARY AND RECOMMENDATIONS

For any country, educational system forms the very backbone of its development. India's education system has been very constantly evolving from the ancient times through different phases such as Vedic literature and the period when Nalanda university and Takshila university was famous worldwide and attracted students from different parts of the world. In the ancient time the education was based on guru-shishya system where class was conducted in open ground. With time modern classrooms evolved and the focus was mainly on teachers, students, blackboard and library. Teachers used to deliver their knowledge either by following books or from their experience. The system do have some own merits such as it provided social exposure of students to other students, students can participate in extracurricular activities with students of same age group and proper guidance from teachers. But with growing population and developments of cities, towns and to deal with various aspirations of a wide range of people having a multi cultural, multi religious and multi linguistics, Indian education system is facing some issues such as lack of quality education as none of the Indian Institute secured a position among the top 100 universities of the World in the Quacquarelli Symonds(QS) ranking, shortage of teachers, the curriculum and the instructional methods are not well developed, unorganised teaching – learning methods, lack of modern and innovative techniques.

Possible alternatives or solutions for interrupted education during Covid-19

- With the help of power supply, digital skills of teachers and students, internet connectivity it is necessary to explore digital learning, high and low technology solutions, etc.

- Students those are coming from low-income groups or presence of disability, etc. distance learning programs can be included.
- To provide support for Digitalization to teachers and students.
- The necessity to explore digital learning platforms.
- Measures should be taken to mitigate the effects of the pandemic on job offers, internship programs, and research projects.
- EDtech reform at the national level that is an integration of technology in the present Indian education system.

We can't ignore that at this time of crisis effective educational practice is needed for the capacity-building of young minds. Central Government and State need to take some measures to ensure the overall progress in the country. Time never wait, this tough time will also pass. Till then stay safe, stay at home!

- The coronavirus pandemic has changed how millions around the globe are educated.
- New solutions for education could bring much needed innovation.
- Given the digital divide, new shifts in education approaches could widen equality gaps.

and financial problems any many others. In such a position our educational system faced another setback due to the COVID-18 pandemic and its social distancing norms. All the educational institutions were shut down and it was made mandatory for people to sit indoor.

To overcome this stressful situation, emerging technology had and can play a great role. The era of 21st century is often regarded as era of technology. Technology plays a very important role in our life as it makes work much more easier and less time consuming. Use of modern technology impact learning very much as it increases the learning and interactivity of students. Internet connection to wide areas has helped students in getting tutorials and other academic helps living in cities, towns, villages and as well as far flung areas. Also the use of projectors and visuals increases the interest level among the students. Students who don't find pen and paper very much interesting they also gets attracted towards the colourful visuals and work that can be done in computer or mobile with the help of technology. Students can get connected with different forms round the clock for assignments and attend webinars or programmes of different institution situated in a different town of even different country from their own house or school. Thus students can get a wide exposure. Students also can avail online degrees from top universities living anywhere in the country. So it helps in increasing the quality as well as the amount of learning in the educational system. Teachers and students can take the advantage of different technological tools to eliminate the drawbacks of the educational system and achieve excellence.

List of technologies available to strengthen online education in India:

Education is a legacy sector, where it takes years often generations to bring about large-scale changes to methods, practices, and operations. While tech-enabled education has the potential to help transform the schooling experience, it comes with certain drawbacks including privacy concerns around misuse of technology, high upfront costs for educational institutions, accessibility concerns, and a lack of training, among others. These barriers will need to be addressed alongside tech adoption in the space.

1. Online learning :

The rise of remote learning amid the Covid-19 pandemic brought the overall online learning industry into sharp focus. As teachers, students, and parents scrambled to grasp remote learning operations following lockdowns and shelter-in-place orders, edtech companies stepped in, either as partners to schools and colleges or as stand-alone replacements.

Even for schools that are choosing to go back to face-to-face instruction, many are adopting a hybrid approach that requires at least some of the course or materials to be held online. In addition to formal learners in grade school or university, adult and post-education learners have also leaned into online learning in the last few years, with Covid-19 accelerating this existing trend. With Covid-19 forcing education to digitize fast, it is hard to imagine a future where online learning is not a core component of education and teaching. Companies are filling in the gaps to meet digital education needs in a variety of ways.

Learning Management Systems:

Learning management systems (LMS) help teachers deliver online lessons, share reading materials, and grade assignments. These platforms can streamline much of the work for teachers by centralizing a number of features on one platform, including the tools needed to run a virtual, hybrid, or in-person classroom, as well as assisting with tracking student progress and connecting with parents.

Massive Open Online Courses:

Massive open online courses (MOOCs) have captured global attention since 2012 when it was projected that they might transform higher education. Globally, several thousand courses are being offered (Coursera, EdX, Udacity, FutureLearn, Udemy etc) and in India, there are the SWAYAM and NPTEL portals. An advantage is that these courses are scalable, they allow for optimal utilization of resources, and being self-paced, are not bound by time constraints.

Massive Open Online Courses (MOOCs) are also seeing renewed interest as a means of gaining higher education. Adult learners in particular are turning to these courses, which are available to anyone with digital access, to fortify their skills or learn new ones to pivot careers.

Afterschool Learning And Tutoring:

Several online platforms provide education that acts as a supplement to learning offered in schools and universities. A number of these after school learning platforms made their services free amid the Covid-19 pandemic to ensure continuous learning for students. These platforms and services can also allow students to get extra help or explore areas that they are interested in on their own time.

For adult learners, online learning might not fully convey the hands-on approach needed in certain fields. While research indicates online learning may help students retain up to 60% more material compared to around 10% in the classroom, it will not be as effective for students who do not have access to the latest technology or who lack conducive environments at home. Learning in physical classrooms will resume once the virus passes, but the partnerships and technology integrations happening today could bring about long-term changes to how we teach and learn. Students may have a wider class selection and more flexibility as they choose between on-site learning, remote learning, or a combination of the two.

2. Virtual and Augmented Reality :

Virtual reality (VR) creates an immersive 3D environment that a user can explore. Augmented reality (AR), on the other hand, superimposes digital elements such as visuals, sound, and text onto a user's surroundings. Both technologies can be leveraged individually or together across education. VR can be used to enhance learning and engagement by allowing students to interact directly with the material. Additionally, AR technology requires the latest smart phones and tablets for each student, and this can be a significant cost for educational institutions.

Other educator concerns include the bulkiness of the equipment, which can be heavy. Some models require a constant source of power to run. In addition, glitches and the quality and availability of content and apps can create problems for educators.

3. Biometrics and facial recognition could help students stay focused and improve safety:

Biometric technology that scans body parts like eyes, fingerprints, and facial features can help identify an individual. On educational campuses, applications could include everything from identifying students to ensuring they are paying attention in class. In addition, the tech can help ensure the security and safety of students on campus. For example, thumbprints can be used to track attendance and alert parents if students don't arrive on time. Facial recognition tech can help track a student's attentiveness through their facial expressions.

The software captures faces of people who enter and exit the school through hundreds of cameras. It then compares the faces with a list of "persons of interest" created by the school. The list includes people with restraining orders against them, employees barred from visiting the school, and sex offenders in the area.

4. Gamification :

Gamification in education is aimed at increasing learners' motivation and engagement by incorporating game design elements such as storytelling, problem-solving, badges, levels, and points in educational environments.

By designing lectures as a game, educators encourage students to face and accomplish various challenges and goals. This promotes higher student engagement and could help students retain knowledge more effectively. It also helps students reframe subjects they may consider burdensome or boring as engaging and fun.

Gamification enables students to receive instant feedback through the use of leaderboards and dashboards that can show how students rank among their peers. This can foster a spirit of healthy competition among students and motivate them to complete assignments to the best of their abilities.

5. Artificial intelligence enables data-driven decisions to increase efficiency and save costs:

The education industry is experimenting with artificial intelligence (AI) applications. Some institutions are using AI to help personalize learning, improve memory retention, teach languages, or increase accessibility to lessons. Companies using AI are not only translating lessons in real time, but are also aiming to assist students with learning languages.

6. Smart campus tech leverages devices and data for a connected experience:

A smart campus is a digitally connected space, where devices and data come together to provide a more intuitive learning experience to students. Devices such as smartphones, laptops and tablets, smart watches, and fitness trackers have become an integral part of people's lives. Among undergraduate students, 95% have access to smartphones, while 91% have access to laptops, according to EDUCAUSE.

However, enabling a seamless operation of thousands of connected devices across campus requires immense technological preparation and planning on the part of the educational institution. Schools need to examine their existing networks and upgrade them as needed to ensure the network can handle a wide range of devices including cameras, sensors, student devices, and more. Colleges also need to ensure that their networks are able to withstand and analyze the vast amounts of data that smart campuses generate.

Opportunities

We are still trying hard to emerge from lockdowns around the world and the toll the pandemic on the education system is taking is tragic. Clearly, a deadly virus is no way to tackle the educational emergencies, but global education standards have fallen sharply as teachers, students and parents have needed to travel and work less, attendance at workplaces has come to zero in all organizations and a fearful environment has emerged all around. Furthermore, much money and other resources are being mobilized to rebuild the robust digital platforms are built to facilitate students' learning, raising the question: can we return back better? Is a sustainable new education system that stops F2F teaching and the experiments in labs in schools possible? What would it look like ahead and how do we get back to our normal teaching and learning? The succeeding points will shed light to answer these questions by turning the current challenges of pandemic into golden opportunities. Classrooms don't teach students: Teachers do. We lack professional teachers. Here is what we should do!

The pandemic has had an indelible effect on the chance to train, upskill, and digitalized the talented learners at a time when they have trouble getting learning their subject knowledge. The final year students and internship holder are anxious and worried about their exams, project and assignment submission, and are investing in the development of their skills and competencies owing to fears of career prospects.

(i) Self-Digitalization: The COVID-19 pandemic has vitally affected countless facets of our lives, particularly the world of education and work. All sectors are grappled with the new-fangled and intricate reality that moved us to use digital tools, platforms, technology, enabled facilities to continue seamlessly to continue our learning. We had incredible talent, enormous potential, state of the art labs and infrastructure, the Covid-19 has augmented the benefits, productivity, and dexterity that digitization can fetch in these terrible and indecisive conditions. The teachers and students have to update, upskill, and learn digital skills to manipulate these unwarranted changes in the way we all used live and work pre-pandemic times.

(ii) Bridge Gaps: The pandemic impact on education has enforced to undertake teaching remotely on digital platforms and gave time to rethink and retool all that we possess and exercise in academia. Along with, the learning outcomes and end results of teacher's professional development have to adjust quickly to the new reality and utilize their skills at appropriate times and places by updating, upgrading, upskilling and reskilling. The teachers and students may take advantage of numerous online resources available, currently offered for free. This would enable and equip them all in their individual capacity and capability to develop their skills and competencies. This induces immense confidence and motivation making ready to grab opportunities in the future.

(iii) Regain pre-COVID Normalcy at Work: Sooner than later, we need to think, plan and execute a phased shift from virtual learning to restart F2F teaching and support the teachers, students, and support staff to return to the school or college. This needs meticulous adherence to new norms of social distancing, sanitization, and face mask at classes. This also needs careful and systematic planning and reviews the safe return to academic plan keeping in view the health impact, hygienic, adjustment in curriculum, schedules, number of students in classrooms, and other operational unforeseen events that need equal attention. With the digital virtual classrooms becoming a reality across the world academia, we have to continue the same for long with technology coupled with minimum disruption on students' learning, motivation and morale leaves little reason for schools to move back to the traditional way of F2F teaching even when normalcy returns.

(iv) Grand Opportunity to recruit Professional Teachers: The pandemic has had an indelible effect on the chance to recruit talented and professional teachers when schools lay off teachers. The institutions can make optimize the time for a quick comeback to excel by shifting priorities to recruit talented teachers. The schools can capitalize on identifying teachers from schools severely affected during this COVID-pandemic. The new teachers will have a lasting impact on students' learning and early recovery. Therefore, we will turn today's opportunities into a reality that will make academics a safe, inclusive, and healthy learning environment to cherish.

(v) Professional Development: The unprecedented and unheard situations have forced to shift from F2F to virtual classrooms requiring digital skills; hardware, software, and technology enable electronic gadgets to cater to students' needs. Teachers had to attain new technical skills in less time while needing more time to address student concerns about assignments, coursework, and final exams remotely. Both teachers and students attend live sessions on online webinars, Zoom, JioMeet, Googlemeet, Cisco Webex, GoToMeeting, Google Hangout, Skype, and YouTube to keep abreast with the latest developments and to have rich interaction with the subject experts. The teachers get insights, precious information on vital topics, teaching methods, use of technology, evaluation and assessment criteria during virtual classes, and cover a wide spectrum of subjects, including effective teaching methods, tips to improve student motivation and engagement. It also attracts inquiry and gives the opportunity to ask questions in the live question and answer sessions. We should acknowledge and appreciate the dedication, commitment, and high degree of adaptability and flexibility of teachers, students, and parents across the academic world.

(vi) ICT Skills Development: Doom and gloom are the two sides of the outbreak coronavirus. On the brighter side, it came with negative impacts, equally, on the hidden side, came up with the boom and fast pace of the digital transformation. This significant change has mobilized teachers for virtual education, training, and opportunities for learners and trainers. The education system in the pre-pandemic was ill-equipped; however, had to shift overnight to online classes. This brought in ICT and training institutions to adapt and flex muscles to meet changes to training faculty, students, and researchers to learn digital skills needed in executing virtual classes. It connects trainers and learners (teachers, students, parents) at different locations, helps to access information anytime, and support the continued professional development of trainers and learners to catch up with the ever-changing ICT skills.

(vii) Students' Transformation to Adapt and Embrace Changes: The students are the worst hit and most affected community from the outbreak of Covid-19. It brought all their activities to halt leaving them in the world of despair, dark, pessimism, fearful, and worried about their exams, family, and career. Long virtual class duration, loneliness, frustration, and no social interaction with friends have also contributed to their worried state. Teachers and school administrators have helped students with accessible information, digital platforms, and necessary software on each of their tabs or computer to enable them to participate in the course, chat, completing given assignments, and quizzes. The situation made them adapt and flexible to the ongoing changes. A few students have created applications and innovative concepts to support and develop the online platform. Today, the students are experts using online conferencing software Zoom, JioMeet, GoogleMeet, Cisco Webex, GoToMeeting, Google Hangout, Skype, etc. Teachers do use them to instruct students in real-time, screen share, text chat to ask questions, monitoring attendance, and file storage for students to upload assignments ensuring instant feedback to all students. Students freely explore digital artifacts and control the specific topic or content classifying them as independent and active learners. The students have complete control of their interactions with media and prompting learner reflection to make them accountable and responsible for the actions bring in more autonomy.

(viii) Adequate Time for Research: The lockdown has brought in both negative and positive aspects for all. It undoubtedly blessed more time to invest in the research work. The study findings showed that more than 46% of survey respondents said lockdown has provided them with more time to "redraft work" and anecdotally, many respondents said they felt far more productive and the lockdown was the best thing to happen to their research. The researchers are traditionally engaged extensively with post-experience students and developed many online delivery applications and methods. The authorities responsible for research should make constructive choices on the policies and practices they adopt to alleviate the pandemic impact, and to consider the long-term impacts on researchers and academia.

(ix) Development of Innovative Practices: Teachers have gained expertise in online teaching using technology and able to create conducive learning environments for effective teaching and learning. The preparation includes contents and activities that are more student-centered, promoting more discussion and collaboration, dynamic participation, self-reflection, active learning, new ways of delivering content, assessing, and providing prompt feedback. They try to develop new instructional skills; tasks encouraging teacher-student interaction and communication required for virtual classroom teaching. The students' online class experience also induces confidence, self-discipline and develops new learning skills they can't develop in traditional classrooms.

What do students miss and wish now?

The sudden great shift to the remote digital platforms due to pandemic has made students anxious, sad, and worried about their future prospects. They suffer from the challenging and unforeseen situations followed arisen from the pandemic and then lockdown and feeling hard to cope with remote virtual learning. The life became monotonous attending long online sessions in four walls missing about going to school, college, and universities: their peers, teachers, discussions and asking questions, visiting library and labs, sports, extracurricular activities. They also miss student-centered learning, interactive lectures, peer-to-peer and student-teacher interaction, thought-provoking discussions and have to bear with many classes synchronously result in considerable lack of motivation, frustration, and disgruntled about their exams and career. Conversely, some students have revealed that they enjoy online classes doing assignments and homework at their own pace, deciding upon their own schedule of study and away from the hustle-bustle and stressful school or college environment. Many a few students residing in remote areas encounter countless challenges of digital and virtual teaching struggling to understand assignments and frequently distracted to not having undisruptive connectivity. Now, they are eagerly waiting for the situation to attain normalcy to resume their academic institutions.

What lies ahead?

The COVID-19 pandemic has shut down the schools and disrupted education systems across the world, underlining considerable gaps that have destabilized students' learning. The unrelenting school closures and many lockdowns have been a wake-up call for all of us to introspect and reflect upon our practices, approaches, resources available, and preparedness to deal with the invisible virus to provide a hygienic and safe environment and protect their rights to education. European Commission (2019) survey had underlined the total lack of preparedness for schools to integrate digital technology in the educational courses, but we couldn't attend to this issue and kept it under the carpet. The probability of viruses staying for long in different forms at different intervals takes us to adopt blended learning to teach students i.e. partially F2F and partially online using the digital platform. Many studies have also shown an advantage for blended learning because both virtual and F2F classroom conditions are different in terms of time spent, curriculum, and pedagogy. Blended learning will provide more learning time and materials along with several opportunities for collaboration. Moreover, online learning leads to the expansion of learning time than in F2F instruction.

Implications for Education

The current research of online and virtual synchronous learning is undertaken to develop research-based insights into online learning practices for students. The researcher went through the previous research on online teaching and the current articles or blogs written on current teaching practices taken up remotely on virtual platforms. The researcher has formulated a conceptual model that can be followed and implemented in the teaching-learning process to make it more effective. Now the administrators and teachers have decided to examine the effectiveness of online learning for different students and subjects and to investigate the effectiveness of different online learning practices. Unfortunately, the extent of the challenge and the work needed to be done to lift students up both academically and socially is a colossus. We should consider it systematically and sincerely to convert the prospect of 'unfinished learning' today to 'complete learning' tomorrow.

Findings

The researcher has find out some important finding regarding this present research as follows:

- There are both positive and negative impact of covid-19 on higher education institutions.

- There are numerous challenges of online education faced by both students and teachers and they adopted some innovative pedagogical skills to overcome these challenges.
- There are both positive and negative effect of online education on students. For this study total 100 respondents participated from five colleges from Siliguri. Impact of online education on students was that maximum (64%) respondents spent their time on educational activities during lockdown period. 90% respondents having android mobile phone as educational resource or e-learning purpose. 38% respondents completing their assignments by own without taking help anyone. 50% respondents find lack of teacher's guidance. 48% respondents satisfied with online classes. Maximum respondents are busy with social media. 78% respondents facing difficulties regarding to find out on line educational resources. 65 % respondents learned new thing from social media for educational propose. 57% respondents thought that lockdown period is very difficult for educational development.
- Both Central and state Governments have initiated various online platform and online courses to overcome these challenges.

Suggestions

In light of this COVID-19 research, the researcher underscores numerous challenges the teachers, students, and parents face triggered a grave concern, conversely, the pandemic has brought many opportunities for colleges and universities around the world to take various actions to protect and ensure the well-being of their students, teachers, support staff, parents and people. The following is a compilation of suggestions based on experiences, observations, and courses of action that schools and colleges have implemented globally. Despite differing in the situation and reality of each academic institution, it is expected that the following measures can provide some glimpses of hope during these crucial and critical times as we continue to learn while we return to the pre-pandemic.

(i) Many universities have been providing quality online education for two decades. The teachers working online should help other teachers with their knowledge and digital skills to design and deliver online course content and assignments.

(ii) We need to learn how to teach and learn with the virus; therefore, blended learning is the most favorite delivery model to be implemented in the future. Educators should get prepared to utilize more time and effort to redesigning existing courses and reflecting on what works better for students.

(iii) The government issues advisory from time to time to deal with the pandemic. The academic institutions follow guidelines on student strength that can be safely accommodated on campus, teaching hours in classrooms, a number of teachers and staff involved attending school, social distancing, use of face mask, campus sanitization, thermal screening, etc.

(iv) Teaching and learning with innovative and effective teaching practices will continue on digital platforms until classes resume the pre-COVID times.

(v) The innovative and new educational approach to a pandemic is a testimony of teachers' dedication, determination, and commitment towards students, parents, and society. It should be encouraged to bridge the skill gap and prepare students with life skills to embrace, adapt, and transform as per prevailing needs and business environment.

(vi) Educators prepare a new-age curriculum matching to fully leverage emerging technologies like artificial intelligence, data science, and data analytics.

(vi) Adequate time to be given to communicating, support students and address their personal and academic concerns

(vii) Establish clear guidelines and policies on courses and programs, contingency plans to deal with COVID like situations and ensure availability of financial funds

(viii) Inform your teachers, students, and parents about the decisions and break the stigma

(ix) Develop and evolve skills through various professional development programs, workshops, conferences, and advice from the experts.

(x) Timely display of leadership skills to ensure the health and security of students; continuity of instructional activities, and programs; upholding academic standards; adaptability and flexibility in finding solutions to the academic and students' problems.

(xi) Always keep your staff, students and parents informed about the latest decisions on the suspension of classes, postponing exams, providing content materials.

(xii) The institutions should prepare teachers who can adapt their pedagogical strategies to make learning more accessible, grasping, flexible, customized, and meaningful, stimulating rather than de-motivating students.

(xiii) Teachers and students should be protected and ensured for security, privacy, and safety issues of using digital platforms.

(xiv) Lastly, the research emphasizes how existing knowledge and learning need to be introspected, reflected upon, reskill, relearn, and update in today's scenario. We must protect our students and provide them consistent and constructive learning for our country, mankind, shared future, and humanity.

COVID 19 has rattled the normal lifestyle of people across the globe; the virtual world has come to the rescue to overcome the crisis. Many institutions, Colleges and Universities have shifted their base to virtual platforms to conduct classes online. Fulfilling to the needs of all stages of education from pre-primary to university level, online education has emerged as an alternative of face to face mode of instruction. Accordingly, various stakeholders such as government and private organizations are trying their best to assist the students to continue their studies. Moreover, efforts are being made by both government and non-government organisations to support the education system through the use of digital tools and applications

In the present perspective of education changes have taken place enormously in every stages of school & higher educations keeping in mind an all round holistic development for children. So the paradigm has shifted to life centred learning from artificial methods. The teacher is now a co learner in the process for the extensive use of modern information and communication tools which are part and parcel of modern teaching learning process. But inadequate scope and barriers in the technological perspective is a major setback in this process. So, in this respect the engagement of students, teachers, and curriculum along with parental involvement is necessary.

1. The following are the provisions made in favour of students.

(A) Stay-at-home learns through online platforms.

Many schools, colleges and universities switched to platforms from the likes of Microsoft and Google along with various conferencing apps such as Skype, zoom for conducting online classes. A shift in the teaching methodology is being observed at-large. Large number of colleges in urban cities made arrangements and trained teachers and educators to teach, communicate and engage with students in online classes. These e-learning programs have been designed to improve communication with each other. While learning through tutorials, video calls, sharing screens and enabling learning software, help students make the most of their virtual learning experience.

According to a report of the Ministry of Human Resource Development, Government of India conducted a survey on higher education and observed that there are 993 universities, 39931 Colleges and 10725 Stand Alone Institutions listed on their portal, which contribute to education. These institutions further reflect the student density of India as the total enrollments in higher education every year are nearly 37.4 million. The switch to online education has been ensuring that students suffer no loss of studies and their progress is being tracked simultaneously with timely evaluation. It is probably a first for India to experiment with the education system and make a paradigm shift to the virtual world, blending classrooms with online learning.

(B) Shift to E-LEARNING

Online learning has become the solution of time and space constraint explicitly. After the introduction of computer communication, electronic learning (e-learning) has been developed based on the basic requirement of delivering content in the digital form to the massive learners conveniently anywhere and anytime the crisis is always paired with opportunities. And it's time to appreciate the full potential of technology for learning. In the wake of this medical emergency and keeping the students' safety in mind along with their academic concern, different have given priority to online.

In wake of the Covid-19 pandemic, students all over the world have been forced to shift to a virtual model of education in schools and colleges.. While the transition has been quite smooth for privileged students, the underprivileged ones are in a pitfall, majorly because of a lack of access to Internet services and electronic devices to view online content, leading to poor and unequal quality of educational services. These unequal levels of access give rise to a digital divide among the students in accessing online education

Thus the online education has become extremely popular, during the onset of Covid19. **Advantages:** The reason why online courses became so popular is because of its multiple advantages over traditional courses. Some of them are:

(A) Online learning can be done anywhere, anytime

(B) Practically even when one is on vacation or on leaves, one can complete a course without having to step out of the home.

.(D) No unnecessary distractions in online courses and learners can complete them at their own pace.

The advantage which is most relevant to the present time is that online courses are safe from the perspective of social distancing. This is the reason why the schools, colleges and universities are employing this method to teach students during the covid19 pandemic. But there are some serious issues and problems acting as barriers in this situation, the most common is the Digital divide across the country.

(C) Digital Divide

Digital divide refers to the gap between those with regular, effective access to digital and information technology, and those without this access. It encompasses both physical access to technology hardware and, more broadly, skills and resources which allow for its use. Factors like gender, physical disability, physical access, age, access to the contents, and lack of ICT skills contribute to the digital divide. Digital libraries can address the issue of bridging the knowledge divide in developing nations, attempt is made to highlight some initiatives taken in India by building digital libraries and bridge this gap refers to the gap between those with regular, effective access to digital and information technology, and those without this access. It encompasses both physical access to technology hardware and, more broadly, skills and resources which allow for its use. Factors like gender, physical disability, physical access, age, access to the contents, and lack of ICT skills contribute to the digital divide.

2.0 Classroom environment is best for learning

However, a physical classroom environment and interaction has been perceived as the best form of teaching-learning method. Though globally, online education has witnessed some success, in India, digital learning would still take time before it is seen as a mainstream learning style. However, the Covid-19 outbreak, and the resultant lockdown, has forced the adoption of digital education amongst the learners.

2.1 The following are the pro's of classroom teaching that digital or online education will find hard to replace:

A. **Promotes collaborative learning** Basically, classroom environment is essential to promote and stimulate collaborative learning. Collaborative learning increases a student's self-awareness about how other students learn and enables them to learn more easily and effectively,.

B. Imcreases critical thinking skills

It enhances students' critical thinking skills. Teaching in a classroom gives students the opportunity to engage in live discussions, debates brainstorming sessions in which they are given opportunity to use their critical thinking skills to formulate opinions, arguments or to solve problems.

C. Improves social skills

Inside a classroom, students experience social interactions with peers and develop respects for teachers cooperation and brotherhood develops among students.

D. Builds organisational skills

Classroom teaching teaches students how to develop organizational skills, beginning with the basics, such as arriving to school on time. In a live classroom, students are held accountable for being prepared to do school work, which includes having done their homework submitting assignments by their due date and being prepared for discussions and interactions..

E. Keeps students stimulated

The physical presence of a teacher keeps students stimulated through the interactive and interesting activities. This enables students to retain more from what they have learned during a session.

F.Teaching style can be modified according to the student's issues

Teachers can modify their teaching style based on learner needs. Teachers can get a clear idea whether students are following what has been taught or they require further explanation. At the same time, students can get their doubts clarified immediately before moving ahead in a topic.

G. Develops important personality and career building skills

Classroom teaching inculcates conflict resolving skills, presentation skills when it comes to presenting their ideas confidently in front of peers, develops team spirit and teaches them to get along with those from different cultural backgrounds. Such experiences are valuable in shaping students' communication and listening skills, as well as growing and maturing emotionally.

As online learning has become more and more popular in the internet era, traditional classroom learning continues to be a tough contender. Despite its advantages, online learning cannot replace traditional education.

However, this alternative medium has also brought to the fore some stark persistent realities of Indian society characterised by social inequalities in terms of availability of resources, essential to access these online classes/platforms. Students and teachers also have their own struggles while accessing these online platforms. Due to financial constraints, students are not able to access the internet, and are devoid of electronic gadgets and laptop, phone or computer or even radio and TV. Those students who have facilities to attend to online classes face barriers in terms of unavailability of physical space, which is equally applicable to teachers who are supposed to conduct online classes from their home.

There are also social barriers such as discrimination against girls as they are expected to do household chores instead of attending online classes in the mornings. In rural areas, boys are often expected to work on the family farmlands.. Most of the time, girls are not allowed to watch educational programmes.

Due to COVID -19 during the lockdown period under graduate students do not have enough educational resource with at their home so that they are worried about their study how to complete assignments, research projects. Another thing they do not have educational tools such as laptop, computer etc. within lookdown period they spent their time with family. Over all they are facing many problems due covid-19 such as educational, family and economically. So, I have suggested the following recommendations to the Government, Institutional authorities and Policymakers:

- It should be made a uniform academic plan for the colleges and also initiate a proper educational plan to continue the learning process during this pandemic.
- The infrastructural facilities should be availed to the educational institutions which can regulate the digital learning process during future health emergencies.
- Availability of electronic device to the learner.
- A strong and steady network system must have to be provided in Dooars area for all success of online learning.

There is a need to ensure adequate funding for the improvement of the education system and to provide capacity development training to the stakeholders of higher education institutions.The year 2020 is going to be most remarkable period of 21st century with millions of death all over the world and degraded economy of countries which are worst affected. Educator sector is also one of the most affected sectors. In this pandemic time regular hand wasting and social distancing or isolation is what we can do.

It is unpredictable that how long it will take to reinstate to the normal situation but till then we have to follow every single precautionary measure. We all know that online education can never replace traditional educational system.

Moreover, digitalized learning gave birth to a new kind of discrimination between those who have access to internet and those who did not have and the main important things that is interaction between students and teachers have also been affected. But apart from the certain challenges and looking at currents situation, online studying is the only option available to students.

Education is indeed the most powerful weapon that can be used to change the entire world, the significance and the necessity of education was realized since Platonic era itself. Today, i.e. in the 21st Century the worth of Education has increased in manifoldsdue to present competitive world where not only education but quality education can completely change one's perspective and can bring developments in the society. In India, Right to Education was enshrined under Article 45 as a Directive Principle of State Policy but via 86th Amendment Act, Right to Education was made a Fundamental Right under Article 21-A of Indian Constitution. The present pandemic has threatened entire education sector and has grossly affected such fundamental Right to Education of students.

According to UNESCO, more than one billion student population has been globally affected due to outbreak of CoViD-19 which has led to shutdown of Schools, Colleges & Universities and has shifted the education to online platform. However, it is not as convenient as it sounds to be, owing to the fact that not every student has an access to technology & internet.

Late Dr. A.P.J. Abdul Kalam in Technology Vision of 2020 and his book *'Ignited Minds'* highlighted the need for intervention of Information Technology (I.T.) in the field of education for transforming the nation into knowledge society with I.T. as the linking tool. The vision of Dr. Kalam has gained more relevance during the present pandemic, however, we are still far from realizing his vision which is evident from the available statistics.

About 66% of the Indian population lives in rural areas and as perthe2017-18 National Sample Survey report on Education, merely 23.8% of Indian households have an internet facility; 14.9 % of rural households have access to internet services and for urban households, the proportion is 42%. For online learning, only access is not sufficient and the ability to use the internet and computer plays equally vital role, it is alarming to note that only 20.1% Indians of age 5 years and above have the ability to use the internet while the proportion of the ability to operate computer is 16.5%.Given the statistics, online education in India is a hard nut to crack.

Proposed solutions: As discussed, there are a plethora of challenges in imparting online education but the pandemic demands such shutdowns, therefore, opting for online means is not a bad idea per se, however, we need to emphasize on removing such barriers in order to facilitate uninterrupted online education for all the students irrespective of their socio-economic status. Such solutions are hereinafter provided in the form of suggestions. Considering the some drawbacks of online classes which have already been discussed above, during a pandemic situation online classes or e-learning is still now the best alternative option of traditional classes that it has proved its merits. In the time of pandemic, online learning is more important so that the education of the students is not hindered. If it can be used effectively, it will enhance the learning process. So, there need to be more educational research and more initiative steps to shake off the disadvantages of online classes and make it more effective. To make it more effective there are some suggestions below:

(a) A combined effort of parent and child: The responsibility of ensuring the safety and security when a child studies at home is on the parent and the child. The parents and the students should take an active interest on online learning. Their combined effort can protect the whole online education system and can make it smart, strong, and safe.

(b) Conduct the examination at right time: As during a pandemic, it badly affects the traditional teaching learning and as well as the traditional evaluation or examination. To test the academic achievement of the students', examination is one of the vital parts of a successful education system. So, there should take more initiative steps to conduct the examination at the right time of an academic year. Also there should take more initiative steps on online examination, so that the every student can take part in the online examination without facing any kind of problem.

(c) Ensuring physical and mental relaxation: As discussed earlier online teaching & learning creates physical and mental problem to the learners as well as the teachers. So, to ensure the physical and mental fitness, there should be a minimum time gap one online class to another.

(d) Come parents and teachers to protect children online: The prolonged access of online brings heightened risks for learner's safety, protection and privacy. So there is a great responsibility to the parents and as well as the teachers to discuss the negative side of internet or online devices with their learners so that they need to be aware of, and what appropriate behavior looks like on the platforms they use, such as video calls in an online learning. There should also be set up parental controls on their devices to mitigate the misuse of online devices, particularly for the younger children.

(e) Ensure the availability of online device and internet: To avoid the discrimination to the students, Governments and as well as the educational institutions should free distribute online devices among the disadvantages students, whose family cannot afford to buy the online devices. The governments and the educational institutions should provide scholarship grant to these students. There should also take initiative steps the accessibility of a moderate internet connection to the every part of the remote areas so that every student can take the advantages of the online platform. The internet service provider should come forward in this regard.

(f) Ensure the online security: As it has been discussed earlier that there are a lot of security issues to using online devices. So the internet service providers, governments and also the education policy makers should give the first and foremost safety priority before rushing to adopting online classes. The cyber security agencies should take more initiative steps to protect the students and teachers private data from the cyber hackers.

(g) Parallel learning: Students and teachers need to get used to online teaching learning. So, the education policy makers and educational institutes should give the same value on e-learning as same as face-to-face learning. Regarding this, there should be the enough value on curriculum so that students can take part parallel e-learning and face-to-face learning. This parallel education may results keep the normalcy in a sudden lock down period.

Suggestions to Government

Right to Education is the fundamental right of every child within the age group to 6 to 14 years which is enshrined under Article 21-A of the Indian Constitution. It is the obligation of the State to safeguard this fundamental right. In order to overcome the challenges in online education like lack of access, inability to use the computer, poor network connectivity, high data consumption, multiple users for single device and financial limitations; the Government should

a. Provide every student with a device like desktop, laptop or tab depending upon the feasibility.Presently, due to Covid-19, India is facing economic set back like rest of the countries across the globe but every problem comes with a hidden opportunity. The Government can collaborate with a national computer manufacturing company like i-ball etc. for providing learning device to the students which will serve the dual purpose of benefitting the students as well as Indian economy by using a device made in India in a true sense.

b. Ensure the availability of good internet connectivity even in remote areas.

c. Ensure that every student has the access to internet and if necessary, to provide free or subsidized internet service for the students who cannot afford internet pack.

d. Frame uniform guidelines on online education, examination, preventing stress regulation of mental health of students etc.

e. Set up more e-libraries with adequate resources for facilitating online learning process without compromising with the quality of education.

f. Ensure proper implementation of Laws dealing with Cyber Crime and if necessary should legislate stricter laws for curbing cyber crimesas students are more vulnerable to such criminals given the time being dedicated online.

Suggestions for Online Teaching

a. Video lectures can be recorded and circulated to the students so that even if there are network issues one can download the same when internet is available and go through it in offline mode. In order to ensure that a student has gone through the video teachers can put up some questions either subjective or objective, in the middle of the video lecture and ask the students to answer through e-mail or Whats app etc.

b. Online classes must be conducted for getting real time experience of classroom learning. However, balance between screen time and online class needs to be maintained which can be done by reducing the duration of online class or by reducing the number of classes per day in such a manner that the screen time for such online class does not exceed two hours. For instance, instead of one hour class for each subject there can be classes for four subjects of half an hour each per day.

c. Classes must be made interactive by holding some discussion session wherein students can actively take part and present their understanding of the topics taught.

d. Apart from syllabus mental health sessions must be held at least once a month by teachersvia zoom/skype/google meet session.
e. Schools and College should work in collaboration with the Government to ensure accessibility to online libraries and research sites
f. Online chatrooms must be created wherein the students can actively take part in interactive session on topics of public importance, or they can share their experiences of CoViD-19, the problems they are facing and the ways they are tackling such issues. It will help the students to calm down and realize that they are not the only one who are facing problems during such unprecedented crises.

Suggestions for Marking

a. Students should be given assignments on weekly basis and marked on the basis of the same rather than conducting one day online examination.
b. Students should also be asked to make video presentations explaining whatever they have understood so as to determine the progress of the student and it will also reflect as to how seriously the student has worked for the assignments.
c. Students can be assigned different topics so that each video presentation can be unique and can be used by one another for understanding a topic.
d. Group assignments must be given to the students so that they can prepare along with their class fellows who will help them to imbibe values like team-work and enjoy learning.

Therefore, by overcoming such barriers coupled with successful structuring of online classes can ensure a constant momentum of online teaching & learning in present testing times. Technology is becoming an important part of our daily life. E-learning, internet and computers have been crucially used in the process of teaching and learning, this research has shown and shown how e-learning and the use of app such as Microsoft Team, Google Classroom, AMIGO, and many others have benefited the students in COVID crisis study at home. The COVID-19 has resulted in schools/college/university shut all across the world. Globally, over 1.2 billion children are out of the classroom. As a result, education has changed dramatically, with the distinctive rise of e-learning, whereby teaching is undertaken remotely and on digital platforms. COVID-19 and the worldwide lockdown have changed the way we look at work and education within a short time. One of the sectors most hard hit by the worldwide lockdown is the education sector. According to UNESCO, over 154 crore students are severely impacted by the closure of educational institutions across the world. In India, private education across the country quickly moved to virtual classes on various online platforms. According to a report of the Ministry of Human Resource Development, Government of India conducted a survey on higher education and observed that there are 993 universities, 39931 Colleges and 10725 Stand Alone Institutions listed on their portal, which contribute to education. These institutions further reflect the student density of India as the total enrollments in higher education every year are nearly 37.4 million, reflecting the expanding horizons of the education industry. The sector was seen catching pace by the passing day until Corona virus impacted the country intensely (Dr. DNS Kumar, 2020).Lack of proper online infrastructure and teaching and non-teaching staff and need to be sanitized the whole educational institution there is too much difficulties to reopen. Further, participation of community, school management committees and local institutions needs to be increased so that local needs and voices are well-represented. Physical distancing, sanitisation and other guidelines for prevention of infection, should be strictly followed for their safety and of others. Siliguri is highly urbanised and one of the concentrated zones that's why it's difficult to continue the educational process and as well as due to the financial crisis its difficult to provide the proper education among the students during this pandemic. (Sing.N, 2020). We need to develop the proper infrastructure for the future to fight against this pandemic more efficiently and without prolonged disruption, as well as move towards building a strong public education system in the country. COVID-19 did teach us how institutions is not equivalent to merely learning, but as a part of a space which belong to a society, a social process, to learn to live, think and act for one's self and the collective good.(Sharma.A,2020) It's never too late to act. Given the current toll and active cases of Coronavirus, remote and online learning will continue for students in at least 2020. We can listen to students and teachers to their ideas and suggestions to evolve our strategies making online content authentic, reliable, more attractive, and easily accessible so as to convert challenges into opportunities eventually empowering students to take charge of their own learning. This would exploit students' full potential as they participate in the actively in-class discussion with the guidance and the tools that make them competent inculcating values, attitudes, skills, and knowledge and critical understanding. We all look to transform the world for the better and should alter social and education, and address old issues of discrimination, poverty, and exclusion. Mankind is worst hit economically, socially, and physically but we should continue imparting education to our talented students. If we unite, the problems get mitigated through solidarity, empathy, and appreciation. For the given reasons, we face really a now-or-never moment. Will academic institutions seize the golden opportunity to reflect on teaching and learning after the pandemic? Let's hope the academic institutions do. Information needs of women as well as their ICT use differ widely. However, there is no ideal ICT that fits all situations. Though women are engaged in numerous roles in agriculture, they are keen to have information on other parts, such as child health, nutrition, prevention and cure of common diseases, employment opportunities etc. Those trying to install ICTs for women empowerment should build their strategies grounded on ICT use pattern and varied information needs of rural women. Emerging a dynamic and relevant content for rural women continues to remain as a major challenge. Adequate resources need to be allocated for this activity, if profits from resources invested in connectivity and hardware have to be copiously realized. Higher education in earlier days was essentially a matter of men of the society. But, today, Government as well as private institutions have come forward for providing higher education to all including women just like men, as per Right to Equality of Education for all, according to Fundamental rights of Constitution of India and are also popularizing higher education further in order to impart quality higher education so that women of every family members can receive higher education in an affordable and effective manner with the new mission to our nation: Quality Higher Education for all women. Although an intra gender inequality, across the caste system was found within the state of West Bengal, in terms of enrolment of women in higher studies, particularly, in job oriented courses, as mentioned above, may be due their social or economic backwardness. However, this was the pre lock down situation which has changed dramatically as it has worked as a catalyst for the educational institutions to grow a new platform with new technologies. This had occurred when among several obstructions, obstacles and restrictions, every country started the action of lockdown to separate the contaminated people, particularly, the young ones of the population (students, pupils etc) by offering opportunities to the education sector to fight to wash away with this present crises so as to survive with a different approach and also to face the present challenge of the threat of the pandemic, only through the path, in order to come out of the rigorous classroom teaching model to a new era of digital model. Not only that, a new approach of technical education of post COVID era also provides a ray of hope of removal of such pre lock down intra gender inequality, as social distancing and online mode of teaching learning process may prove this in future. Let's hope for the best. Education is a country's lifeline and basis for its development. Like any other sector such as health, defence etc education should be given equal importance and share in the investment as today's investment will yield a better result tomorrow. India's education system through these years has evolved a lot but needed more revolutionary changes and Government's New Education Policy has helped in it. It has increased the investment in education sector by allotting a greater share of GDP. It has also changed the pattern. Increased use of technology in the classroom and academic setting will yield a positive result with this new policy. During the lockdown period for COVID-19 , online learning as served as the educational lifeline by keeping the learners and educators engaged and safe by maintaining social distancing norms. Only providing technology will not help, teachers are needed to be provided training in how to use technology and to promote it among students. Technology is needed to be made available and used to the fullest to provide the appropriate and effective learning to students. High speed internet connectivity should be ensured to all people specially disadvantaged groups and low income families. Modern tools and technology increases the learning and interactivity because the transfer of knowledge becomes very easy and it makes study very interesting as was being evident during the very testing time of this pandemic. Though there are some demerits of online learning but its merits are much more in number than the merits and the demerits can be overcome with the help of evolving technology. Safety and safeguard measures need to be evolved more. Covid19 situation taught us how extent the importance of using technological tools and online platform for teaching learning. Different types of natural of disaster motivate us for more thinking on virtual learning by using various e-learning tools (Tull et al., 2017). The development of Science and technology reached its optimum level but in question of control of nature, it kept silent. Each and every year different natural disaster will came and we just prepare ourselves for this. Technologies in that time will likely help us for cope with them (Meyer

& Wilson, 2011). So, It is undeniable the contribution of technologies in education even in the time when other education providing system lost their hope. This pandemic situation taught us that know, understand and use of technologies will give most priority from the future. We need to ready for acquire the master on using e-tools which can help us for facing any types of challenges. Govt. should give the priority for ensuring equity and equality for easy access of information communication technology by giving the internet connectivity in rural and remote areas, smart phones availabilities, smart classroom infrastructure etc by which students can smoothly continues their online classes, video chat, learning in online platform (Zoom, Edmodo, Google classroom), webinars, web conferences etc. Along with the face to face teaching-learning. So a combined teaching learning approach will more necessary for 100% participation in education with more innovative methods. It can be concluded that teachers, students, and parents all are affected by the online learning directly and indirectly. Online learning is full of merits and demerits. Some people are enjoying the benefits of online learning while others are frustrated by the demerits of it. But rest of the people who are capable to afford the technology, but they lack the knowledge of online learning. Besides this, online learning or digital learning have their own technical faults and many other issues. The country is suffering from the mastery knowledge of technology. In spite of being many demerits of online learning .It has the administrative power for moving the nation towards development and progress. People have got the opportunity to update themselves through online learning. It has overcome the turmoil condition of the education sector due to the covid-19. If there is no opportunity to foster online learning then the plenary of pour country including education has reversed backward for a long time. Both teachers and students have achieved the mastery of technology. To make the online learning effective and productive to all the education related people, government has taken many fruitful steps and initiate more than one platform to fulfil the dream of the nation. A number of adjustments have to be made to both instructional modalities and to the curriculum in order to implement useful, relevant and effective online courses. Changes to the curriculum typically revolve around several key points, which include- deciding upon and structuring learning activities; selecting the readings and the other course work upon which the learning activities would be based; allocating enough time for learning activities to be learned; ensuring that changes created by any actions taken with respect to all of the above are relevant to the remainder of the course content. Modifications to instructional approaches imply both the conversion of effective traditional instructional strategies into purposeful online practices and the acquisition of new knowledge and competencies in a number of technologies and pedagogical areas. Effective online teaching strengthens and extends course objectives and changes the process by which students meet these objectives and learn course content. The power of online course lies with the professional educator's ability to create a student-centered learning environment where each student engages in the active construction of meaning, drawing upon myriad internal and external factors affecting students learning in online environments. COVID-19 will be with us for a long time. The current situation has accelerated our use of digital technology and can transform our education system for the better. There is also no looking back from here. It is essential that the government should invest more in education, health and research sectors. Special funds need to be allocated for digitization and to raise digital learning platforms. The private sector also needs to participate, and should enhance research capability in order to develop proposed solutions. Finally, it is essential that the government offer financial support to all students in order to lessen the digital divide. Face-to-face interaction in classroom teaching will take time to return, and almost surely, it will return with new norms such as a blended mode, or with changes in student-teacher ratio so as to maintain proper social distancing. Meanwhile we can use this time to experiment and deploy new tools and technology to make education meaningful to students who are not able to go to campuses. We can also devise plans to increase access – *Education for all* – in both rural and urban areas.

From the above discussion it may be sum-up that any kind of pandemic is an unpredicted and untold terrifying situation to a large geographical area of the world. Its sudden impact on education may lead the whole education system to a major challenge. In the midst of this digital world we should take the advantages of the digital technologies to keep an uninterrupted and unhindered teaching-learning system and normalcy in the whole education system. Online education is one of the greatest example and dimension of the digital technologies. Amid the crises time in a lock down period online education, has come as a panacea. During the pandemic instead of halting the process of education, virtual learning or e-learning is the best alternative option of face-to-face learning , as it adheres to the norms of social distancing as laid down by the governments as a precautionary measure against the spread of the virus. However, there are some drawbacks of online education which has been discussed earlier. Each mode of learning has its own merits and demerits. It can be undoubtedly say that in the time when people have to stay at home during a pandemic situation, online learning has a great positive impact on students' education. So, if we can overcome the drawbacks, the online learning truly may be the panacea to the world of education during the crisis period in the pandemic situation.

Suggestion to make online teaching better-

1. Record your lectures-don't stream them-if students are unwell or struggling with internet excess, they will miss a live stream lecture. Record videos instead and send them to your students so that they can watch in their own time.

2. Show your face- research has shown that lecture videos that show instructors faces are more effective than simple narrated slide shows. Intersperse your slides with video of yourself.

3. Keep video short- videos longer then fifteen minutes can cause issues of slow downloading and learned distraction. If you have more to say, record two or more short videos.

4. Test out slides- make sure you test slides on a smart phone before shooting your lecture's so all text is readably on small screens. Font sizes, colours, template designs and screen ratios can be double checked.

5. Use existing resources- it is unrealistic to expect that you, on your own, will produce a semesters worth of high quality videos. You can use pre-developed resources available online and provide students with clickable links.

6. Use open access points- using open resources help prevents access problems for students. If any of your suggested resources are not accessible, you will receive an inbox full of student emails and eventually waste all your time trouble shooting. Spending a few extra minutes carefully searching for fully open access materials will save you headache latter.

7. Give specific instructions- when you suggest online media which runs for longer than fifteen minutes, students will be put off watching instead, suggest that exact parts they need (eg 13:35 to 16:28) as this can even make students more curious. When you provide more than two resources, label them in order you want students to approach them. Simple numbering based on the level of difficulty or importance of each

resources item, can be of great help for your students.

8. Provide interactive activities- most learning management systems, such as Moodle, Edmodo and Blackboard, include a range of functions to create interactive learning activities such as quizzes. Sept –by –step guides to creating them are widely available online. Use them,

9. Set reasonable expectations- when you create quizzes, you should make sure all questions can be answered by referring to a given learning resources. When you ask students to write a summary of lecture videos, you should make it clear that this is not a serious report. Making this as a mandatory assignment bet a low-stakes task will produce the best outcomes and responses from students. A set of 15 quiz questions or a 300-word limit will be sufficient to engage students for 30 minutes

10. If you tell students that their attendance will be measured by their participation in quiz, it will increase compliance. However, you won't have to check them all, so use the automatic checking and grading features on learning management systems.

11. Group communications shouldn't be used for direct teaching. Instead, set up "virtual office hours" on a video conferencing too like Zoom. Simply log in at the appointed time and wait for students. Focus on providing social support and checking if any issues need to be addressed immediately. This can be a great to collect student feedback on your online teaching as well. Make meetings optional and be relaxed. No need to be frustrated when no one shows up: students are still happy to know that this position is available.

12. You can set up online group spaces for small group of students and ask them to support and consult with one another before sending emails to you directly. You can post a couple of questions to help students break ice and start conversation. Encourage students to use the communication tools to prefer. Some groups will click well and some will not, but this little tip can make students feel socially supported and reduce your inbox traffic.

13. Online teacher's emotional openness is a great instructional strategy. Tell your students that it is your first time teaching online and you are learning while teaching. Explicitly ask them to help you, reassuring them that you will do your best to support their learning as well. They will be sympathetic since they share the same emotions, and you will be set up for success.

14. Online students do not like frequent changes in their learning styles. They are happy to repeat the same structured and activities. Once you find a teaching style working for you, feel free to repeat it each week until you are back in your classroom.

Recommendations

The curriculum should give more focus on the Information and communication technology in demanding and primary level of education. Government should more focus on implementation rather than new more programs are launched. The government will organized the different ICT programs in the frequently interval of time sphere. So that the society can easily accepts the new technology and its importance. Training, workshop may be organized a regular or short interval of time basically in rural areas of the country. So the teacher and teacher educator raise the half efficacy, self-esteem, irrespective of their higher education. Develop a quick response mechanism process to monitor program towards ICT development in rural areas.

Every individual should be empowered by augmenting their skills, understanding creativity and access to information technology equally in rural and urban region. Central government gives equally response in internet among the people.COVID-19 is a disease caused by a new strain of corona virus. 'CO' stands for corona, 'VI' for virus, and 'D' for disease. Formerly, this disease was referred to as '2019 novel coronavirus' or '2019-nCoV.' The COVID-19 virus is a new virus linked to the same family of viruses as Severe Acute Respiratory Syndrome (SARS) and some types of common cold. The emerging infection of COVID-19 was initiated from Wuhan, China, have been spread to more than 210 countries around the globe including India. The clinical symptoms of COVID-19 are very similar to other respiratory viruses. The number of laboratory-confirmed cases and associated deaths are increasing regularly in various parts of the World.

The COVID-19 is an emerging viral infection responsible for pandemics. Fortunately, the mortality of COVID-19 is low as compared with SARS and MERS, the majority of its cases are recovered. The death toll of COVID-19 is high even after its low mortality because COVID-19 causes a pandemic while SARS-CoV and MERS-CoV cause epidemics only. COVID-19 influenced the large segments of the world population, which led to a public health emergency of international concern, putting all health organizations on high alert

The outbreak of coronavirus disease (COVID-19) has been declared a Public Health Emergency of International Concern (PHEIC) and the virus has now spread to many countries and territories. While a lot is still unknown about the virus that causes COVID-19, we do know that it is transmitted through direct contact with respiratory droplets of an infected person (generated through coughing and sneezing) Individuals can also be infected from touching surfaces contaminated with the virus and touching their face (e.g., eyes, nose, mouth). While COVID-19 continues to spread it is important that communities take action to prevent further transmission, reduce the impacts of the outbreak and support control measures. The protection of children and educational facilities is particularly important. Precautions are necessary to prevent the potential spread of COVID-19 in school settings; however, care must also be taken to avoid stigmatizing students and staff who may have been exposed to the virus. It is important to remember that COVID-19 does not differentiate between borders, ethnicities, disability status, age or gender. Education settings should continue to be welcoming, respectful, inclusive, and supportive environments to all. Measures taken by schools can prevent the entry and spread of COVID-19 by students and staff who may have been exposed to the virus, while minimizing disruption and protecting students and teachers.

Bibliography

Agarwal, S., et al, (2020), Effect of COVID-19 on the Indian Economy and Supply Chain, Preprints, doi:10.20944/preprints202005.0148.v1.

Annual Report (2009-2010), Ministry of Education, Government of West Bengal, wbhed.gov.in.

Aggarwal, J. C. (2010). Teacher Education in a Developing Society (5th Edition). Noida, Uttar Pradesh: Vikas Publishing House Pvt. Ltd.

Affouneh, S., Salha, S., N., & Khlaif, Z. (2020). Designing quality e-learning environments for emergency remote teaching in coronavirus crisis. Interdisciplinary Journal of Virtual Learning in Medical Sciences, 11(2), 1–3.

Adedoyin, O.B., & Soykan, E. (2020).Covid-19 pandemic and online learning: the challenges and opportunities. *Interactive Learning Environments, pp- 1-11,* DOI: 10.1080/10494820.2020.1813180. *Retrieved from* https://doi.org/ 10.1080/ 10494820. 2020.1813180

Arkorful, V., & Abaidoo, N. (2015). The role of e-learning, advantages and disadvantages of its adoption in higher education. *International Journal of Instructional Technology and Distance Learning*, 12(1), 29–42

Athar, U. & Sharma, G. (2020). Parents, teachers scramble for access to e-learning in rural india. Retrieved from https://www.livemint.com/news/ india/parents-teachers-scramble-for-access-to-e-learning-in-rural-india-11593948421008.html

Aung T.N, Khaing S.S (2015) Challenges of implementing e-learning in developing countries: A review. *International Conference on Genetic and Evolutionary Computing. Springer*, Cham; 2015. p.405-411

Alqurashi, E. (2018). Predicting students' satisfaction and perceived learning with online learning environments. Journal of Distance Education, 40(1), 133-148.

Bonnel, W. (2008). Improving feedback to students in online courses. Nursing Education Perspectives, 29(5), 290-294.

Barboni, L. (2019). From shifting earth to shifting paradigms: How webex helped our university overcome an earthquake. CISCO, Upshot By Influitive.

Basilaia, G., Dgebuadze, M., Kantaria, M., & Chokhonelidze, G. (2020). Replacing the classic learning form at universities as an immediate response to the COVID-19 virus infection in Georgia. International Journal for

Research in Applied Science & Engineering Technology, 8(III).

Briggs, B. (2018). Education under attack and battered by natural disasters in 2018. TheirWorld. https://theirworld.org/

Carey, K. (2020). Is everybody ready for the big migration to online college? Actually, no. The New York Times. https://www.nytimes.com

Chan, C., Chen, N. S., Cui, W., Hu, X. et al. (2020). Handbook on facilitating flexible learning during educational disruption: The Chinese experience in maintaining undisrupted learning in COVID-19 outbreak. Smart Learning Institute of Beijing Normal University.

Cathy.L & Farah.L (2020) The COVID-19 pandemic has changed education forever. This is how , 28 april,2020, retrieved from https://www.weforum.org/ agenda/2020/04/ coronavirus education-global-covid19-online-digital-learning/

Dewi, W. A. F. (2020). Dampak Covid-19 terhadap implementasi pembelajaran daring di Sekolah Dasar. Edukatif: *Jurnal Ilmu Pendidikan*, 2(1), 55-61.

Dhawan.S (2020) Online Learning: A Panacea in the Time of COVID-19 Crisis, *Journal of Educational Technology Systems* 2020, Vol. 49(1) 5–22 , 2020

Daniel, S.J. Education and the COVID-19 pandemic. *Prospects* (2020). https://doi.org/10.1007/s11125-020-09464-3

Das, K.K. et. al., (2020), The Impact of Covid 19 In Indian Economy – An Empirical Study, International Journal of Electrical Engineering and Technology (IJEET), Vol. 12, Issue 03, pp.194-202.

Das N.G., (2013), 'Statistical Methods', McGraw Hill Education (India) Private Limited, Vol-

1&2, Ninth reprint.

Favale, T., Soro, F., Trevisan, M., Drago, I., & Mellia, M. (2020). Campus traffic and eLearning during COVID-19 pandemic. Computer Networks, 176, 107290.

Gupta, S. (2005). Education in Emerging India (2nd edition). Delhi: Shipra Publications.

Jena, P. K. et. al., (2020), Impact of Pandemic Covid-19 on Education in India,International Journal of Current Research, Vol. 12, Issue 07, pp.12582-12586.

Kumar, c, & Sachdeva, M. S. (2010). Vision of Secondary Education in India in the Context of 21st Century (1st edition). Patiala, Punjab: Twentyfirst Century Publication.

Kumar, S., et. al., (2020), Impact of coronavirus (COVID-19) on Indian economy, Agriculture & Food: E-Newsletter, Vol. 2, Issue 04, pp.300-302.

Gunawan, G., Suranti, N. M. Y., & Fathoroni, F. (2020). Variations of Models and Learning Platforms for Prospective Teachers During the COVID-19 Pandemic Period. *Indonesian Journal of Teacher Education*, 1(2), 61-70.

Kama, A.A. et al. (2020). Transitioning to Online Learning during COVID-19 Pandemic: Case Study of a Pre-University Centre in Malaysia. *International Journal of Advanced Computer Science and Applications*, Vol. 11, No. 6, pp- 217-223. ISSN: 2156-5570 (Online). Retrieved from Transitioning to Online Learning during COVID-19 Pandemic: Case Study of a Pre-University Centre in Malaysia (thesai.org)

Khalil. R. et al (2020). The sudden transition to synchronized online learning during the COVID-19 pandemic in Saudi Arabia: A qualitative study exploring medical students' perspectives. *BMC Medical Education, vol-*20 (285), pp- 1-10, https://doi.org/ 10.1186 /s 12909-020-02208-z

Liguori, E. W., & Winkler, C. (2020). From offline to online: Challenges and opportunities for entrepreneurship education following the COVID-19 pandemic. Entrepreneurship Education and Pedagogy. https://doi.org/ 10.1177/2515127420916738

Littlefield, J. (2018). The difference between synchronous and asynchronous distance learning. https://www.thoughtco.com/ synchronous-distance-learning-asynchronousdistance-learning-1097959

Li, Q., Guan, X., Wu, P., Wang, X., Zhou, L., Tong, Y., Ren, R., Leung, K. S., Lau, E. H., Wong, J. Y., & Xing, X. (2020). Early transmission dynamics in Wuhan, China, of novel coronavirus–infected pneumonia. New England Journal of Medicine, 382, 1199–1207. https://doi.org/10.1056/ NEJMoa2001316

Meyer, K. A., & Wilson, J. L. (2011). Online journal of distance learning administration (vol. IV, no. I). University of West Georgia, Distance Education Center

Mishra, L. et al. (2020). Online teaching-learning in higher education during lockdown period of COVID-19 pandemic. *International Journal of Educational Research Open*, Vol- 1 (2020), article no- 100012, https://doi.org/10.1016/j.ijedro.2020.100012

Moazami F, Bahrampour E, Azar MR, Jahedi F, Moattari M. Comparing two methods of education (virtual versus traditional) on learning of Iranian dental students: a post-test only design study. BMC Med Educ. 2014;14:45.

https://doi.org/10.1186/1472-6920-14-45

Mayadas, A. F., Bourne, J., & Bacsich, P. (2009). Online education today. Science, 323 (5910), 85-89. https://dx.doi.org/10.1126/science.1168874

Mkrttchian, V. (2011). Use "hhh" technology in the transformative models of online education. In G. Kurubacak & T. Vokan Yuzer (eds.), Handbook of research on transformative online education and liberation: Models for social equality (pp. 340-351). Hershey, PA : IGI Global. https://dx.doi.org/10.4018/978-1-60960-0464.ch018

Moreno-Ger, P., Burgos, D., Martínez-Ortiz, I., Sierra, J. L., & Fernández-Manjón, B. (2008). Educational game design for online education. Computers in Human Behavior, 24(6), 2530-2540. https://dx.doi.org/10.1016/j.chb.2008.03.012

Cochrane, K. (2016). Transformative learning in online professional development: A program evaluation (Ph.D. Thesis). College of Professional Studies, Northeastern University, Boston, Massachusetts.

Eom, S. B., Wen, H. J., & Ashill, N. (2006). The determinants of students' perceived learning outcomes and satisfaction in university online education: An empirical investigation. Decision Sciences Journal of Innovative Education, 4(2), 215-235.

Gaytan, J. (2015). Comparing faculty and student perceptions regarding factors that affect student retention in online education. American Journal of Distance Education, 29(1), 56-66.

Kuo, Y.-C., Walker, A. E., Belland, B. R., & Schroder, K.E.E. (2013). A predictive study of student satisfaction in online education programs. The International Review of Research in Open and Distributed Learning, 14(1), 16-39.

Lone, A. Z. (2017). Impact of online education in India. IJESC, 7(7), 13050-13952.

Parvathi, K. et. al., (2019), Indian Economy During Indira Gandhi's Regime-A Study, International Journal of Social Sciences Research and Development (IJSSRD), 1(2), pp 36-42.

Pandey, P. (2018). Educational technology and ICT in Education (1st edition). Kolkata, West Bengal: Rita Publication.

Ray, R. (2020). ICT in Women Education. In D. Subba (Ed.), Integrating ICT with Education (pp. 109–120). New Delhi, India: APH Publishing Corporation.

Rathore, Singh and Dubey, Barriers to Information and Communication, Technologies Encountered by Women Sponsored by The

Commonwealth of Learning and the British Council, November 26 – 28, 1998, India

Rieley, J. B. (2020). Corona Virus and its impact on higher education. Research Gate. Save the Children. (2014). No child left behind, Education in crisis in the Asia-Pacific Region Victoria.

Rieley, J. B. (2020). Corona Virus and its impact on higher education. Research Gate.

Saxena, K. (2020). Coronavirus accelerates pace of digital education in India. EDII Institutional Repository.

Singh, V., & Thurman, A. (2019). How many ways can we define online learning? A systematic literature review of definitions of online learning (1988-2018). American Journal of Distance Education, 33(4), 289–306

Shaik, G. and Babu, P. R., (2018), Micro Insurance -Mechanism and Opportunities for the Sustainable Development of Indian Economy, International Journal of Mechanical Engineering and Technology, 9(2), pp. 857–865.

Tull, S. P. C., Dabner, N., & Ayebi-Arthur, K. (2017). Social media and e-learning in response to seismic events: Resilient practices. *Journal of Open, Flexible and Distance Learning*, 21(1), 63–76.

UNESCO IESALC (2020). COVID-19 and higher education: Today and tomorrow. Impact analysis, policy responses and recommendations. Retrieved from http://www.iesalc. unesco.org/en/wp-content/uploads/ 2020/04/COVID-19-EN090420-2.pdf

Zogas S, Kolokathi A, Birbas K, Chondrocoukis G, Mantas J. (2016) The e-Learning Effectiveness Versus Traditional Learning on a Health Informatics Laboratory Course. Stud Health Techno Inform. 2016;226:109–12. https://doi.org/10. 3233/978-1-61499-664-4-109.

UGC 12th Five Year Plan on Higher Education, Chapter 7, ''Enhancing Quality and Excellence in Higher Education,'' Pg 87.

Verma, N. et. al., (2018), Initiatives of Government of India to Boost up Indian Economy. Journal of Management, 5(4), pp. 496–503.